SONAL
MANSINGH

Sujata Prasad

SONAL MANSINGH

A Life Like No Other

PENGUIN
VIKING

VIKING

USA | Canada | UK | Ireland | Australia
New Zealand | India | South Africa | China

Viking is part of the Penguin Random House group of companies
whose addresses can be found at global.penguinrandomhouse.com

Published by Penguin Random House India Pvt. Ltd
7th Floor, Infinity Tower C, DLF Cyber City,
Gurgaon 122 002, Haryana, India

First published in Viking by Penguin Random House India 2017

ISBN 9780670089277

Typeset in Adobe Garamond Pro by Manipal Digital Systems, Manipal
Printed at Replika Press Pvt. Ltd, India

www.penguin.co.in

Contents

Author's Note

I met Sonal on a cool evening on the cusp of winter at her home in Defence Colony, Delhi, in 2012. It was two days to Diwali and the trees leading to her place were corseted in gold lights. When she opened the door, it was evident that the charm that had transfixed audiences in the 1960s, '70s and '80s was still intact. She offered me a drink, steering me towards a Lebanese red wine from the Bekaa Valley. The evening crackled with energy and playful humour.

I recalled seeing her on a stage in 1994 or 1995, slathered in a slew of lasers as Draupadi. Violated on every score, Sonal's Draupadi still seemed strong enough to be the misogynist world's worst nightmare. It was difficult for me to take my eyes off her then, as it was now.

A little sloshed by now, I was pure gush. I asked her if I could write her biography. I had taken a few months of study leave to research a book on the political economy of Bihar, but could shelve it if she said yes. She was completely non-committal. She doubted my seriousness.

We continued to meet in stunning settings, and only sometimes in banal ones. For me, every meeting was a cinematic moment: walking by the quirky eateries and alternative stores of Hauz Khas Village, picking up hippy chic, her long necklace snaking into her décolletage; meeting her at the salon at The Ashok, a chatty masseuse by her side; seeing her break the celebrity bubble at random concerts and cinemas; early morning at the ITC Windsor in Bengaluru, watching her eat her bowl of granola and eggs on toast, silhouetted against a window; eating myself to death at her place while watching her delicately peck at her food.

Initially, I would go to meet her wherever she invited me, happy to share a slice of her evening, exploring key ideas that have shaped dance or even discussing random, unexceptional stuff with her. There were many Sunday afternoons spent in existential musings and abstract ruminations. I had no idea where all this was leading. At best, I seemed to be gravitating towards a book obsessively preoccupied with the history of India's classical dances.

I can't remember when the narrative changed over the course of our meetings, and she began to look back at her life. We walked down five years of the memory lane, sometimes ten, teetering deliciously between a no-holds-barred account and a bunch of evasions and omissions. I learnt to feel my way through her thoughts, reconstructing her past through not only a bricolage of conversations and media reports, but also her parables and spells of silence.

I also realized that Sonal is not cagey about her personal life. There is something immensely disarming about her candour. At seventy-two, she is as sharp, fun, cheeky and fallible as an adolescent, constantly seeking moments of beauty and renewal—a complete one-off free spirit, her boldness always ahead of its time, even in 2016.

There is an edge, a brittleness to her, an oversensitivity to criticism, a hardwired sense of what is right, a certain hauteur. She can be outspoken, cocky, when one least expects it, but most of the other commonly held perceptions about her are completely off the wall.

It's incredible just how many drafts and how much artifice it takes to tell a story such as hers. I was tempted to create novella-like chapters by shoehorning our conversations into a part-fact, part-fictional tale. Sonal gave me a rap every time I breached the borders of the real and the imagined, and insisted on getting her story and her voice right. She also set limits on how much I could probe, not caring about the narrative dead zones that would stare at us periodically. What helped were her sharp intellect, her incredible wit and the unexpected tenderness with which she handles her memories.

My obsessive redrafting and conversational longueurs were more than a little tedious, even for me. I spent several unproductive months corralled into a tiny writing space, staring at jottings in different notebooks. It's a wonder that Sonal refrained from having me walled up alive.

1

Born to Dance

For a woman born in 1944, Sonal looks incredibly young. It was in 1944 that a country eviscerated by years of colonial domination went as if into labour. The most dramatic event that preceded Sonal's birth in a hospital in Bombay[1] was an explosion at the Bombay harbour on 14 April in which hundreds of lives were lost. Wartime and commercial cargo valued at £20 million went up in flames. This included enormous amounts of gold bullion in bars that is said to have hurtled across the ravaged dock area in a shower of gold.

For the Pakvasa family from Gujarat, the birth of their 'golden girl'—Sonal—on 30 April was the redemptive aspect of this bizarre tumult. There is a picture of her as a toddler, sitting in her paternal grandfather's lap, his face blissed out with the joy of holding her. Her grandfather, Mangaldas Pakvasa, was a close confidant of Mahatma Gandhi. A successful solicitor, he was a man with a razor-sharp intellect, adorably warm and compassionate, who touched innumerable lives. When he joined the freedom movement during the Salt Satyagraha in March 1930, he donated his entire personal wealth to the movement, embraced khadi, even went to jail several times. He was president of the Bombay legislative council between 1937 and 1947.

Sonal's mother, Poornima, was part of a feisty group of new-wave women seizing life with both hands in the frenetic political and social landscape of colonial and postcolonial India. Born in 1913, in Ranpur near Limbdi in Saurashtra[2] to a family of freedom fighters, she was one of the thousands who waded into the edge of the ocean with Gandhi during the Salt March and scooped up a handful of salt. This was on 5 April 1930, a day that marked the end of a 241-mile non-violent protest march against the colonial government's salt monopoly. Barely seventeen when she was jailed for subversive defiance in Rajkot, Poornima shared her mouldy cell space with Kasturba Gandhi. The time spent together in prison laid the foundation of a lifelong relationship with Gandhi and Kasturba.[3] Poornima left the maelstrom of active politics when she married Sonal's father, Arvind, a quiet, behind-the-scenes political worker who later became a renowned philatelist. She remained attuned to the metaphysical aspects of Gandhi's thought and ideas— embracing them in their totality later in her life. Gandhi's idea of how free India should be structured became her talisman.

In 1945, a year after Sonal was born, the Second World War ended. With this, the colonial empires started crumbling. Britain pulled out of India in 1947. The birth pangs of a free nation resulted in intense political and cultural convulsions. The air was alive with endless possibilities. Sonal's family was at the centre of these convulsions. Mangaldas Pakvasa was appointed governor of the Central Provinces and Berar (present-day Madhya Pradesh) in 1947, followed by terms as governor of Bombay and Mysore.

Sonal's childhood was spent in the razzle-dazzle of beautiful, old, foliage-drenched Raj Bhawans[4] at Nagpur, Bombay and Bangalore, and in a spacious, rented family apartment at Malabar Hill. Her early life had all the ingredients of a fairy tale. One of her earliest memories is of her adorable little rag doll, Cheebi. She also recalls with great fondness the thrill she felt in riding an elephant from the Nagpur airport to the Raj Bhawan on the eve of Independence, escorted by Bhima, a family retainer who remained part of the household till he died. A quieter thrill when her father's sleek new Chrysler equipped with rare car luxuries arrived in Bombay. And at twelve, the thrill of smiling into the eyes of the Dalai Lama,[5] dressed in a taffeta frock with faux pearl buttons!

For Sonal and her siblings, it was extraordinary exposure. Jawaharlal Nehru, Sardar Patel, C. Rajagopalachari, Rajendra Prasad and many other contemporary leaders would visit their home for long political discussions. Their home was also a hub of poets like Ramdhari Singh Dinkar and Chandravadan Mehta, leading writers like Jyotindra Dave, scholars, and leaders of different faiths, all of whom would engage in fiery intellectual and cultural exchanges.

Sonal was the antithesis of her quiet siblings—elder sister, Arti, and younger brother, Anuj. There were endless scrapes and escapades, with her grandfather as her ultimate backup. He was always there for her, no matter what. By the age of four, she was already a little fighter, fiercely independent, a powerhouse of confidence. Behind all her pranks, her grandfather could sense the nerves of steel, the quiet determination. He took a great deal of pleasure in mentoring her. She was *sonya dikro*,[6] his special one, with an irresistible gamine charm. It was an idyllic time when she would do everything she could to get his attention. The only time he turned ballistic was one witheringly warm day when, annoyed with someone who was combing out the knots in her hair, she shut herself in an old wooden cupboard and went off to sleep. The cupboard somehow got locked. For some time, no one noticed. An hour or two later, her grandfather, eager to take her along for an event, noticed that she was missing. A massive search operation was launched. She was finally found curled up on a pile of blankets, her eyes heavy with sleep. She was walloped by her grandfather and remembers crying her eyes out.

Sonal inherited her musical genes from both her parents. Her mother had a bachelor's degree in music from the SNDT College (Shreemati Nathibai Damodar Thackersey Women's University) in Bombay and took lessons in Manipuri dance[7] from Guru Naba Kumar Sinha. Sonal's father was a musician of rare and subtle talent. He learnt classical percussion or pakhawaj and was adept at playing the *dilruba*, an instrument that is a cross between a sitar and a sarangi.

Sonal's own formal lessons in classical vocal music began when she was eight. Her gurus were Professor K.G. Ginde, an eminent scholar and composer, and Dr Sumati Mutatkar, a vocalist and musicologist of the Agra gharana.[8] She also learnt to play the sitar from Deb Burman, a disciple of Ustad Vilayat Khan—and later took lessons in Carnatic classical vocal music from Sri Venkataraman. Sonal's long years of training in classical music opened up a musical universe that she has been exploring ever since.

Sonal's passion for dance was ignited at the age of four, when her parents arranged classes in Manipuri with a teacher in Nagpur. Born to dance, she was a quick learner and danced with a passionate intensity rare for that age.

My teacher's name was Robin Roy. I would rush back from school, gulp down a glass of milk and eagerly await his arrival. My lessons were planned three times a week, but any occasion for me was good enough to get dolled up and take a few turns and receive fond applause from the audience. When I was a little older, I would dance my heart out, forgetting that I needed to stop.

It was not a generation that was pressed for time, and Sonal was encouraged to make the most of the time at her disposal. Which she did, auditioning for school productions and giving sweet, homespun performances at celebratory events at the Raj Bhawans and pirouetting to danceable music. Like most little girls, she also dreamt of becoming a pointe-shoed ballerina and has starry-eyed memories of being taught foxtrot and waltz by General Cariappa (later the first field marshal of India) on a family holiday in Kodagu.[9]

I remember being drugged with happiness as I twirled and hopped and giggled in the arms of the handsome general.

The Raj Bhawans were venues for music congregations or *baithak*s where legendary classical singers would congregate. Just as interesting as the music was the line-up of Pakvasa kids,

5

who sat around listening intently—their musical tastes shaped by a childhood spent in baithaks.

Our appetite for music was inexhaustible even at that young age. Sitting cross-legged in the Durbar Hall of the Raj Bhawan, our heads would gently roll to sleep, only to be woken up again by the strains of a *tarana* or thumri.[10]

Sonal remembers Siddheshwari Devi, one of the finest exponents of thumri, cradling her in her arms affectionately and calling her *Sona Bai*. Pandit Omkarnath Thakur, a towering presence in Hindustani classical music and a frequent visitor from Kashi, was treated like a *nana* (maternal grandfather).

The great maestro Bade Ghulam Ali Khan was another frequent visitor. Accompanied by his son, Munawar Ali, on the tanpura,[11] and brother, Ustad Barkat Ali Khan, on the harmonium, he loved treating the audience to seasonal melodies—singing Raga Malhar when it rained, his *gamak taans*[12] accompanying claps of thunder. He lived a block away from Sonal's parental home in Bombay. Sonal remembers waking up to the sound of his awe-inspiring thumris floating across Malabar Hill. Then there were legendary names like Ustad Faiyaz Hussain Khan, sarod maestro Ustad Hafiz Ali Khan, and the senior Dagar brothers, Moinuddin (an iconic *dhrupad* singer) and Aminuddin, who were invited frequently for concerts. M.S. Subbulakshmi,[13] in her gorgeous sarees and jewels, hair perfectly coiffed, was also a frequent performer.

Sonal shared a special relationship with Moinuddin Dagar and his wife, Suraiyya. They loved the young firecracker, bright and outspoken, and encouraged her to pop in frequently at their home near Bhulabhai Desai Institute in Bombay. At their place, she was fed home-made delicacies and treated to unforgettable music. Dagar's astonishing vocal range never ceased to amaze her. She was also awestruck by Suraiyya's beauty.

She was certainly one of the loveliest women I have ever seen. Daughter of a nawab's family of Lucknow, she was also immensely talented and played the tanpura in all his concerts.

Sitar maestro Ustad Vilayat Khan was another frequent visitor at the Pakvasas' Bombay home.

I remember their small, charming flat on Napean Sea road, where he lived with his Bengali wife, Monisha, and toddler son, Shujaat. His daughters were not yet born. I used to visit them frequently, hoping to catch him during his practice of *gayaki ang*,[14] in which the microtonal inflections of the sitar would magically replicate the human voice.

Pandit Jasraj gave one of his first vocal recitals on Sonal's twenty-first birthday, guided by his brother, Pandit Maniram. Pandit Jasraj had just moved from being a tabla accompanist to a full-blown vocalist. He sang the poignantly romantic raga,[15] Kaunsi Kanada, much to everyone's delight.

It was a big moment. We all knew that he was destined to create great music.

Sonal studied at the Fellowship School, an institution with a strong, uncompromising vision of what a school should do. In a strict, Gujarati-medium, academic environment where music, dance, painting and the study of Sanskrit were compulsory,

Sonal made her mark. She remained focused on her academic curriculum while excelling in dance and music. In class, when a teacher asked a question, without exception, her hand was the first to be raised. Her linguistic precocity never ceased to amaze her teachers, as did her refined visual sensibility, her use of imagery and metaphors, her perfect pitch in a school choir, her breathtaking, liquescent dance moves in her stage debut as Ram in a ballet on the Ramayana.

An active girl scout, she participated in the All India Scouts and Guides Conclave in Jaipur in December 1959.

I had graduated to being a girl guide—very proud to be following in my grandfather's footsteps. His pooled effort with Pandit Nehru, Maulana Abul Kalam Azad, H.N. Kunzru, Pandit Sri Ram Bajpai and Vivian Bose had led to the merger of the splintered Scouts and Guides organizations in November 1950. He was the national president of the merged organization known as Bharat Scouts and Guides. There was a plethora of activities rolled out for us at the conclave and I remember plunging into them with great gusto despite freezing every night in my tent in an open field, where we were all housed.

It was not all serious, though, and between classes, there was enough time for the rough and tumble of regular childhood—time to play *kho-kho*,[16] *kabaddi*,[17] and a game with stones called *nargoliyo* even in lashing monsoon rains; time to slip out of the school gates to buy forbidden tamarind and raw mango flakes and eat them with salt and red pepper; riding home in trams and on the B1 route in a BEST double-decker . . .[18]

Sonal recalls the revelry during Janmashtami[19] celebrations with great fondness.

We girls were a rowdy lot. We enjoyed shouting and screaming as we helped boys make a pyramid. The wolf whistles and catcalls all came from us. We would jostle the boys and push them to the ground many times before allowing them to reach the earthen pot full of white butter and coins. The deal was that boys could eat the butter but the coins were to be handed over to us girls. Our wrath fell on whoever chose to cheat us. And then followed the extended rounds of the suburbs with my parents and siblings to cheer, scream, jostle and shove, our clothes liberally splattered with mud and butter.

Sonal also had a wonderful talent for mimicry and was her school's stand-up comedian. There were countless uproarious moments. She remembers troubling her Sanskrit teacher and deliberately rubbing him up the wrong way with her quirky renditions of Sanskrit idioms. She loved caricaturing him and others, like her music teacher, Pandit Bhimrao Shastri, a quaint old man always dressed in a Banarasi topi,[20] dhoti[21] and a long coat, with a fondness for *itr*, the traditional Indian perfume. Despite this, even the most crotchety among the teachers loved her.

Sonal's pranks aside, hers was a childhood spent conforming to the rules of the Pakvasa household. While her parents were not really uptight, there was no time for trivia or gossip and certainly no sleepovers with friends. Sonal had to play by her mother's rules at most times, whose strict regimen was only occasionally offset by her grandfather.

We were a spirited lot, piling into our car at a moment's notice to catch a show at the Regal or Eros cinemas; or for a picnic at Juhu beach with our cousins and friends; driving down the 3-kilometre stretch along the sea from Malabar Hill to Chowpatty to Nariman Point; stepping down for an ice cream on the promenade at Marine Drive and a ride in horse-driven Victorias.[22] And then there were the art events, dance and music concerts, at many of which my grandfather would be the chief guest. I saw my first Kathakali performance in the company of Bharatha K. Iyer, the great exponent of this classical Indian dance form, whose book on Kathakali[23] is a landmark.

Sonal was at her outrageous best at dinner, when, to the accompaniment of delicious Saurashtrian food[24] cooked by Jetha Maharaj and later Ram Jivan, their family chefs, she would regale the family with stories of her real or imagined peccadilloes. This was followed by raucous moments in the big, noisy room she shared with her siblings, and quieter moments with her *Maasi Ba* (mother's maternal aunt) in a small adjoining room where all her secrets would come tumbling out. This room was also her refuge during holidays. It was brightly lit with an outdoorsy feel, a place for dreamy, picnic-like interludes and romantic, oneiric fantasies.

One foot in childhood, the other in adulthood, Sonal was an incandescent beauty. She was blitzed by attention wherever she went, most of all at her sister's wedding with businessman Dhananjay Mehta in December 1959, but she did not really care. There was something else that had completely possessed her by then. Dance!

After school, Sonal joined Elphinstone College for her undergraduate programme in German, attracted by the syntactic beauty of German literature that she had discovered in her bibliophile grandfather's library. The large collection had some new, some dog-eared books, copiously underlined. There were books that she read obsessively many times over—prized first editions of books by Dr Kanaiyalal Maneklal Munshi, a political activist, writer and educationist, and Jhaverchand Meghani, a writer, poet and social reformer, books by Goethe, Brecht and Thomas Mann in beaten-up hardcovers and paperbacks . . . She fell in love with Goethe's exquisite poetic sensibility, reflected in the English translation of poems like the 'Wanderer's Nightsong'—'*Uber allen Gipfein*'—poems set to music by Franz Schubert. She craved to read everything in the original language in which it was written.

* * *

We are in Sonal's book-lined home, eating theplas[25] *spiced with fenugreek, and charred, smoky aubergines.*

'Describe your teenage years,' I ask her.

Well, they were kitschy and teenage *(laughs)*. I was slowly moving away from a sequestered life. I had long, thought-stoking conversations with my grandfather, unstitching history, literature and philosophy. There were also intimate bondings with friends with all the cloying sentimentality of adolescence. I remember writing letters filled with anecdotes to two of them—Asha Nanavati and

11

Soni Bagai. And the third was my Spanish friend, Bettina de' Almeida, an aspiring dancer with whom I went saree shopping, buying blush pinks, shades of orange, fiery reds with jewel-toned *kanjeevaram*[26] borders for performances. I was already steeped in the arts, hence time was a precious resource, infused with a sense of purpose. Dance was my gateway to adulthood.

You were a stunning teenager. A free spirit. You must have had more than a bunch of admirers.

Was I a free spirit? Far from it! I did not cruise around smoking weed. There were boys who made outrageous attempts to flirt with me, but I continued to live in some kind of a pre-pubescent fog. I was naïve to the point of being stupid. At college, I mostly hung out with girls of my age. Life did not move only around coursework. I engaged with student issues, participated in sit-ins, developed a hybrid vocabulary of different art forms. Altogether too busy for romance! Many, many years later, Jyotindra Jain,[27] an undergraduate student at St. Xavier's around the same time, confessed that he used to frequent Elphinstone just so he could look at me, as did many others. I was oblivious to all this at the time.

You never had a routine, assembly-line life, not even when you were in school?

When I was in school, politics was the wallpaper of my life. Yet, in many ways, we were also brought up as absolutely ordinary children. Let me share an anecdote with you. I visited Delhi for the first time in 1948 with my grandfather, who had been invited for the first governors' conference. We stayed with Sardar Patel at his official residence on Aurangzeb Road. When Sardar Patel and my grandfather were leaving for the conference at the Rashtrapati Bhawan, his daughter, Maniben, was told to give us children some toys to keep us happy and engaged. Maniben laughed and said, '*Ji Bapuji*, I have already organized live toys—the mali's and driver's children are here, and as soon as you leave, they will be engaged for the whole day.' And that's how simple it was.

We improvised games with whatever was around. I am sliced through when I see my young students flaunting their smartphones and other gadgets. I grew up with Gandhian values and the non-slavish, liberated spirit of a free, young nation. Consumerism passed us by.

You were very close to your grandfather, weren't you?

Yes, extremely. His public persona never came between him and me. He was the only one who could deal with my teenage histrionics. He could shut me up by saying, '*Natak shoon kare chhe?*' ('Why are you being theatrical?'). Incredibly open-minded, he stood by me at all times, and I would like to think that I have inherited from him his fierce sense of self-respect and fighting for what is right. He will remain an inspiration all my life, and is present even in his absence.

Did he support your decision to be a dancer?

Yes, absolutely. He had some reservations initially. I remember throwing a few tantrums. I sulked for three days—no food, no conversation. It did not take him long to be convinced that it was the right decision, a credible one. He did make me promise to treat dance as worship, but that was all. He understood my choices. He accepted them even during unexpected, life-altering events. I remember an incident in 1964, just after my debut recital in Delhi. I was staying at Morarji Desai's place since he was a close family friend. My plan was to learn a few precious *padams*[28] from Swarnasaraswati, the immensely talented sister of Balasaraswati,[29] during my extended Delhi visit.

Fortunately, when I arrived in Delhi, Morarji *kaka*,[30] who was then finance minister of India, was away on a tour. I say 'fortunately' because, in some ways, he was a tyrant, rigid in his likes and dislikes, wary of the performing arts. One morning, when I was leaving for my class, I saw that he was back and was leaning over his spinning wheel to spin. This was his daily morning ritual. I went up to him and touched his feet. He blessed me and wanted to know where I was going. When I told him, he was furious and tried to forbid me from going, saying that my dancing would bring disrepute to my family. I freaked out! When he found that I was in no mood to listen, he called up my grandfather. Far from admonishing me, my grandfather told Morarji kaka that I should not be censored, nor should any limits be imposed on what I wanted to achieve as a dancer.

And your parents? You had a somewhat fractious relationship with you mother, didn't you?

My father indulged and spoilt me. He was part of my ice cream escapades near the Flora Fountain. He taught me to be a water baby. With him I could be wildly exuberant, even bordering on the anarchic. He remained one of my closest friends till his death in 1995.

My relationship with my mother was rarely on an even keel. When I was growing up, it was natural for her to have some amount of parental anxiety. I was strong-willed, obdurate, given to occasional house-rattling tantrums— an understandable source of consternation! In dealing with me she was somewhat of a tigress. I was thrashed by her often, but was never expected to conform to a quiet, doll-like version of femininity. She herself grew up in an environment that was free from rigid, patriarchal social constructs. Both my sister and I were raised to be equal to boys.

She had an incredible life. She met Mahatma Gandhi when she was eight. That chance meeting more or less defined her life. My grandfather saw her as a volunteer in half-pants and shirt during the fifty-first session of the Indian National Congress at Haripura, a village in Gujarat, in 1938. She had an electrifying presence which seemed at odds with her bravura display of precision and control in dealing with a mammoth crowd of more than half a million. My grandfather was convinced that she would be the most appropriate as my father's life partner. My mother did not make up her mind immediately. She came to live with them for a month. My father was an only child, so, for a month, my father and grandfather were on probation.

She was far ahead of her time and found her niche in development work in the Dangs, a poor tribal district of Gujarat. This resulted in a lifetime's struggle to provide nutrition, education and vocational training to tribal girls from impoverished families.

Your mother seemed to know that you would be a dancer.

Yes. When she was pregnant with me she saw Uday Shankar perform in Bombay. His visually rich choreography that took the best from traditional Indian dance forms and European ballet movements absolutely fascinated her. She could also feel me respond to the dance music in her womb! The lingering tenderness of those wondrous movements remained with her for a long, long time.

You once told me that, since childhood, your mind has been awash with imagery of water.

I love water and have been greatly fascinated by this primal element in creation. It can feel like velvet or a knife, translucent like the moon, shining like a mirror, and suddenly dark and foreboding, heavy with the secrets of creation. My affair with water began when I was just four years old, when my father swam through a pool in Pachmarhi carrying me on his back. Since then, I have swum in flowing rivers, in lakes and oceans.

My river experiences include swimming in the Narmada at the historic temple town of Maheshwar, in the river Krishna when it was in spate following heavy rains in Jamkhandi, in the Tungabhadra near Hampi, in the Yamuna at Vrindavan, at the sangam[31] in Prayag and in several other small and big rivers and streams in different countries.

One of my most enduring memories is of white-water rafting on the Ganga many summers ago. On a sudden impulse, I jumped off the raft much above Rishikesh, somewhere close to Brahmpuri, floating past temples, ashrams and ghats, and chanting shlokas to propitiate the Ganga, feeling the incredible thrill of gliding across many walls of water. I managed to berth on the sandy banks near Lakshman Jhoola, much to the amazement of my co-rafters and the chagrin of the tour operators.

My ocean experiences include swimming in the chilly water of the Atlantic at Ogunquit, in the warm waters of the Indian Ocean at Kanyakumari, in the icy waters of the North Sea. Another unforgettable tryst with water was in the oil-like, soft, caressing water of the Adriatic at Dubrovnik.

Did water ever intimidate you?

No. I would like to think that my father had a big role to play in my love for water, no matter what. But the closest I came to drowning was when I swam in Lake Michigan in Chicago. The Indian consul general had invited me for a picnic on a lovely, sandy beach, and I enjoyed a perfect swim. A fortnight later, during another outing at the same place, I ran into the water humming a tune. Not for long! A rogue undercurrent began to pull me down to levels where the water was icy beyond belief and where other rogue currents were waiting to grip my limbs and pull me down further. I had drifted so far away that no amount of shrieking would reach those on the shore. Providentially, I was swept close to thick wooden logs, and held on to one with all my strength and then managed to swim back to safety.

Your parents brought you up to admire Indian classical music.

I was brought up with a strong sense of my cultural heritage and roots. But I am passionate about all kinds of music, from Kishori Amonkar, the doyenne of the Jaipur-Atrauli gharana to folk music from all corners of the world. I like listening to Bob Dylan's 'Blowin' in the Wind' and other songs. I loved Elvis Presley when I was a teenager, his jumping around and acting the fool, his intensity when he sang songs like 'Are You Lonesome Tonight'. I adored Pat Boone's 'Love Letters in the Sand'.

Any raunchy, coming-of-age memories?

No. Just some pre-pubescent crushes when I was aching to grow, and some innocent kissing and canoodling as a teenager. But yes, I think I was a little in love with my German professor, in college. I now suspect that one of the reasons I decided to study German was his good looks and dashing style.

Ever felt the pressure to conform?

No, I was lucky I was not stuck in a provincial space or a dead-end life.

2

The Bharatanatyam Years

Tai tai taam
Tai yum tat ta
Tai ha tai hi

Sonal cut her teeth as a Bharatanatyam dancer when she was barely seven, repeating the beat of the *tattakazhi*[1] with the clap-like sounds of her naked feet on the hard floor of her guru's house, her tiny hands rehearsing one of the twenty-eight single-hand gestures known as *asamyukta hasta mudra*s, followed by twenty-four joint-hand gestures, her fragile arms in perfectly synchronized positions at the ankle, chest, shoulder and above-head levels. Her guru, Kumar Jayakar, a disciple of the legendary Meenakshisundaram Pillai, trained her in yoga for several weeks and made her do cartwheels and other arduous exercises on her toes while fully seated or half-seated, before beginning on the *adavu*s, the basic units of the dance form.

Etymologically, the name Bharatanatyam is derived from its four most important dimensions—*bha* from *bhava*,[2] that is *abhinaya* (gestures), *ra* from raga or melody, *ta* from tala or rhythm, and finally *natyam*, meaning dance. A quaint story explaining its origin dates back to prehistoric times. Gods and goddesses pleaded with Brahma to create a non-esoteric fifth Veda[3] that could be easily understood even by a commoner. Acquiescing to the request, Brahma took *pathya* (words) from the Rig Veda, abhinaya from the Yajur Veda, *sangeet* (music) from the Sama Veda and *rasa* (emotions) from the Atharva Veda to form *Natyaveda*—a comprehensive text on the knowledge of dance, music and theatre. After completing the *Natyaveda*, Brahma handed the treatise to sage Bharata and asked him to popularize it. Bharata then wrote the scholarly text, *Natyashastra*, the epic science of dramaturgy. The grammar and aesthetics of Bharatanatyam, perhaps one of the oldest of classical dance forms that continues to exist in contemporary India, is traced to this treatise, written between 200 BC and AD 200.

Sculptural evidence, in the form of beautifully carved dance postures known as *karana*s, has been found at the Brihadeeswara temple at Thanjavur, the Nataraja temple at Chidambaram and the Sarangapani temple at Kumbakonam, indicating that variants of this dance form were used extensively in temple worship. There is a reference to dance in surviving literary texts from the Sangam era, such as *Tolkappiyam* and *Silappadikaram*.

The temple precincts supported devadasis,[4] a matrilineal community of dancers, tied in ritual bond to the temple deity, their nuptials marked by the *pottukattu* or the *taali*-tying ceremony. Devadasis sang and danced an older version of Bharatanatyam, known as *Sadir Natyam*, *Dasiattam* or *Chinna*

Melam, passed from one generation to another by *nattuvanar*s.[5] Sadir Natyam was also performed in the courts of kings and princes, and for other royal connoisseurs and aficionados.

There seems to be a broad consensus that the repertory danced in contemporary times was codified in the late eighteenth and early nineteenth centuries by four extremely talented brothers—Chinnaiah, Ponniah, Sivanandam and Vadivelu—who were star performers at the royal courts of Thanjavur and Travancore. Known as the Thanjavur Quartet, the brothers were renowned scholars and musicians credited with refining the music of Bharatanatyam, influenced by their mentor, the iconic composer, Muthuswami Dikshitar.

In 1838, a group of devadasis performed in Vienna, Paris and London. Their bewitching dance aroused considerable interest in oriental traditions. Sadir Natyam suffered a severe setback during the second half of the nineteenth century and early twentieth century when, coloured by Victorian sensibilities, public opinion against it gained ground. The dance, once considered sacred, came to be seen as having become mired in an overdose of eroticism, and was described in appallingly sexist, pejorative terminology as nautch.[6] Dancers, especially those who were courtesans, were pilloried and had to deal with an incredible amount of outrage. A bill was piloted in the Madras legislature to abolish the devadasi system in 1928. Evidence however suggests that *arangetrams*[7] continued in temples of Pandanallur and other places until the anti-nautch legislation was passed in 1947, four months after India celebrated its first Independence Day.[8] What an irony!

Despite its impending evanescence, Sadir was nonetheless kept alive by an active underground of nattuvanars and devadasis, who learnt to stoically square up to lacerating barbs. Veenai Dhanammal, a highly accomplished Carnatic musician, ran a weekly Friday salon for dancers, musicians and art connoisseurs in Madras. A month-long salon during the Rama Navami festival was hosted by another important patron of the performing arts, Ramaniah Chettiar.

Resistance to the suppression of Sadir surfaced from unexpected quarters. E. Krishna Iyer, a freedom fighter and lawyer, donned female devadasi attire and began performing the dance in public spaces, fighting contempt and condescension through his essays in newspapers and magazines on the aesthetic dimensions of Sadir. Several scholars, musicians and critics pledged their support to Sadir. Iyer also played an important role in founding the Music Academy in Madras in 1928 and using its platform to encourage devadasis to perform, loosening in the process the noose of fear and inhibition.[9]

Recontextualizing the dance by moving it from public festivals, temples and courts to a concert stage was a major game changer. Several devadasis used the Music Academy stage to perform, beginning with a concert series in 1931. The long list includes eminent dancers like the Kalyani sisters, Balasaraswati, Mylapore Gowri Ammal, Varalakshmi, Saranayaki, Bhanumati, Nagaratnam, Muthuratnambal and Sabharanjitham. The gravitas they brought to the dance began to turn hard-core sceptics into admirers. Sadir Natyam was rechristened 'Bharatanatyam' by the Academy. The first official use of the name can be traced to 1933.

At the vanguard of this resistance were young, educated girls from elite, conservative Brahmin families who learnt Bharatanatyam and then performed defiantly on the Music

Academy's stage, brewing a storm that swept anti-nautch tirades away. People who had earlier turned their noses up at the dance form now came to the performances in droves. Rukmini Devi Arundale's debut performance at the Adyar Theatre on 30 December 1935 grabbed unprecedented media attention[10] and silenced the remaining detractors.

> Rukmini Devi's contribution to Bharatanatyam is too vast to be articulated in words. She worked on refining its aesthetics. She choreographed new items within the *margam* format,[11] including *varnams*[12] and padams,[13] introduced devotional lyrics known as *kritis* in its repertory. She was probably the first to dance under proper stage lighting. She refined the costumes and accessories, finding a way of reining in the excesses. One of her greatest contributions was orchestrating a move away from the *guru–shishya parampara*[14] model of sustained study with a single mentor by establishing the Academy of Arts, Kalakshetra, in 1936. She broke a traditional male preserve by introducing women to *nattuvangam*, the joy of conducting dance.

Of the devadasi performers, Mylapore Gowri Ammal and Balasaraswati were the most visible in terms of their performances and the role they played to accelerate Bharatanatyam's revival and outreach. Balasaraswati, the immensely talented daughter of Jayammal and granddaughter of Veenai Dhanammal, belonged to the seventh unbroken generation of a family of temple dancers and musicians. Trained by the legendary Kandappan Pillai, she took Bharatanatyam outside its ghetto in Madras when she performed in Calcutta and at the All India

Music Concert in Kashi in 1934, beginning her international chapter with the 'East–West Encounter' Festival in Tokyo in 1961. Both as a performer and a teacher,[15] she was at the centre stage of the international dance milieu along with eminent dancers like Margot Fonteyn, Martha Graham and Merce Cunningham, who were smitten by her incredible body of work. Performing essentially within the solo margam, she was described as one of the supreme performing artists in the world by the *New York Times'* dance critic, Anna Kisselgoff.

Then there were dancers like the Michigan-born Esther Luella Sherman who changed her name to Ragini Devi, and Bruce Murray Turner, who did their best to ensure that Bharatanatyam was recognized as an important performing art form. So was Ram Gopal whose contemporary stagings were a rage in London's West End theatre, and Uday Shankar who used Bharatanatyam movements, costumes, and instruments like the mridangam and the veena to place Indian dance on the world map.

Sonal's teachers during her formative phase were the most sought-after—Professor Ubhayakar Shivaram Krishna Rao and his wife, Chandrabhaga Devi. Uncompromising in teaching the grammar of the *Pandanallur bani*[16] that they had imbibed from their guru, the legendary Meenakshisundaram Pillai, her gurus were unconventional in more ways than one. To begin with, they broke the glass ceiling in the face of absolute opposition from their conservative Konkani Brahmin community when they went to Thanjavur to learn dance from their guru. Professor Rao was a professor of chemistry at the Central College, Bangalore, and played cricket for the star-studded Bangalore United Cricket Club. He was later appointed honorary professor of dance at the university.

Sonal learnt Bharatanatyam in their dance school, Maha Maya, every summer, when the family moved to Bangalore to spend time with her grandfather who was governor of Mysore state at the time.

> My mother took me to their school and asked them, 'Will you accept her?' They were non-committal initially. It was only when I demonstrated what I knew that they said they would take me. I was not accepted immediately just because I was the governor's granddaughter.

In Bombay, Sonal continued her training at the Bhulabhai Institute, and later at the Chitrambalam Dance Centre founded by Jayalakshmi Alva, one of the foremost disciples of the renowned guru Dandayudhapani Pillai.[17] Learning at the Bhulabhai Institute was rewarding in more ways than one. A centre of visual and performing arts, it was a meeting point for creative personalities like the Dagar brothers, Ravi Shankar, M.F. Hussain, Gaitonde, Dashrath Patel and others. Amir Khan, the much-admired khayal[18] singer, was often spotted there under a pipal tree doing his *riyaz*.[19] Sonal's friendship with sitar maestro Ravi Shankar started here, as did her acquaintance with Waheeda Rahman[20] and Jabeen Jalil, who were also Jayaben's students.

> Those were amazing days. People now can't even imagine what the atmosphere was like then. It was a moveable feast! Mumbai was also a hub of jazz musicians—jazz was a part of my university's cultural consciousness, and many of my Goan and Parsi college-mates were followers of

Chic Chocolate, Mickey Correa, Leon Abbey and others. Music was in the air—one just had to walk past the Flora Fountain to Bistro and Volga for an evening charmingly soundtracked by piano, guitar, bass and drums.

Sonal's arangetram took place in 1961 at the white-and-gold darbar hall of the Raj Bhawan at Bangalore, in the presence of her grandfather, who was the acting governor of Mysore, her parents, musicians, eminent dancers, scholars, and celebrities like the Maharaja of Mysore and Devika Rani Roerich, the first lady of Indian cinema. The arangetram is a coming-of-age event in the life of a Bharatanatyam dancer, which also finds a reference in the Tamil epic, *Silappadikaran*.

> Having taught the prescribed format called margam, which includes the repertory from *alarippu* to *tillana*[21]—a process that takes seven to twelve years of training—the guru makes preparations for the formal presentation of the pupil to the dance world. This event is known as arangetram or *rangapravesh*—where *ranga* means 'stage' and *pravesh* is 'entry'. If the assembled critics and connoisseurs judge the student to be worthy of a future as a dancer, she can continue her training with the guru. Thereafter, she can also appear in stage performances, usually at the discretion of the guru.

For Sonal, it was baptism by fire.

The run-up to the arangetram stretched her in ways she had not anticipated. It involved rigorous practice sessions, sequestered for hours in a small room. Her gurus demanded perfection, and could be hard as nails. One of her favourite anecdotes is related to a practice session on a hot May afternoon, during which she was expected to combine a technically impeccable performance with the dramatic intensity of abhinaya. The context was the portrayal of a young woman desperately in love with Shiva. Sonal had to distil the essence of *sringara*[22] and create a magical moment dripping with sensuality, love and devotion. It was past noon and she was exhausted. Her face remained bereft of emotion, tiredness writ large on it. 'Try harder,' her guru exhorted, 'eyes softer. Bend your stupid head and look up from under the eyelashes at the form of Shiva. Don't frighten the poor god away.'[23]

> Tears come easily. My face remains in a fixed expression of non-comprehension. We have been working at polishing the centrepiece of the Bharatanatyam repertory—the varnam. It is the most complete, complex and demanding piece of living art ever invented! I have got the thirty-five-minute framework of the varnam firmly etched in mind with all the *jathis*[24] and *swaras*[25] and their corresponding movements. Body is ready and raring to dance. Even the text in Telugu, with meanings of words and context, is committed to my photographic memory. But what of this face which refuses to plead, yearn, pine?!

The much-needed jolt came in the form of a juggler who appeared outside the open window and contrived to make a couple of monkeys dance. Prof. Rao pointed his tattakazhi in their direction and asked her to establish the difference between the monkeys and her.

'Show me the difference between the monkey and you.' This was certainly a kind of a watershed moment—I learnt a very important lesson, an unmissable one, turned up my pitch and delivered what was needed. My guru's scepticism was completely scotched by my performance.

During her two-hour arangetram, Sonal danced exuberantly, her expressions shaped by an unusual dramatic intensity. She began with an invocation and moved through the entire margam with ease, executing the rhythmic improvisations with verve and certitude, ending the recital with an enchanting tillana.[26]

The local newspapers covered the event with a flattering portrayal of the young dancer, her technique and abhinaya. A Kannada daily commented on her grip on *angika abhinaya*[27] and her beautiful, expressive *satvika abhinaya*,[28] and said that she had kept the audience completely immersed in a flow of emotions for the entire duration of her performance. Art critics and reporters were equally appreciative of her incredible beauty, the clear luminosity of her skin, the delicate symmetry of her features, her lotus-like eyes, her lissom figure.

The verdict of the examiners, eminent scholars like E. Krishna Iyer and G. Venkatachalam, came two days later when they were invited to a ceremonial meal at her guru's house. A number of questions related to the theory of Bharatanatyam were directed at Sonal.

One wrong answer and I would have been disembowelled by my gurus, but I managed to get my answers right and my gurus and everyone present that evening had nice words for my technique and abhinaya.

A small, unfussy celebration followed.

* * *

We are in Sonal's svelte little study, being followed by the penetrating eyes of Bhagwati from a Purulia Chhau[29] *mask in her living room.*

How did you manage to remain grounded while receiving praise from the likes of E. Krishna Iyer?

It was not like today, when Facebook walls and Twitter feeds can turn you into an instant celebrity. For me, it was just the beginning of a long, creative journey. My upbringing, my gurus, were enough to rein in the hype.

Many dance scholars have written about the amateurization of arangetrams.

My arangetram involved gruelling practice sessions, sometimes up to six to eight hours a day, seven days a week, for weeks on end, in a small room or an improvised auditorium. For me, it signified the end of one phase of my training. I took the flurry of attention in my stride and continued to practise.

Soon after that, you ran away from home.

It was clear to me that I would have to write my own script. At my arangetram, the Maharaja of Mysore and Devika Rani and others told my parents and my grandfather that

I was made for dance and dance alone. Any hopes that I would follow a beaten path were already foregone.

I had no Plan B and wanted to take no chances. There was no concept of a gap year then. I had just finished my graduation. My grandfather's tenure as governor was over and he was back in Bombay. But even with his support, I did not expect a tectonic shift in the attitude of my parents. My decision to be a professional dancer was attracting a fair amount of opprobrium. There was a vast disconnect between their expectations from me and my own dance-related aspirations. So finally, I did what I needed to.

I used the scholarship money obtained for a postgraduate programme in a German university for my secret journey to Bangalore. I left home rather dramatically, packing my essentials in a Girl Guide bag and an old holdall, and slipping out to take a BEST bus to the Victoria Terminus station. From there I took a train to Pune, changing to a metre gauge train to Bangalore, and finally a rickshaw to guruji's home. It was all very theatrical!

Imagine the surprise of my gurus! They returned from a film to see me sitting bedraggled at their doorstep. The headlights of their small Morris Eight blinked twice before they came out to embrace me. By then, my grandfather had lodged a missing person's complaint with the police and was so relieved when guruji called him that he forgot to be angry with me.

Were you homesick?

No. There were no aches or longings. Even at that age, I had the tenacity and willpower to do what I wanted. My gurus had been a part of my dance life for what felt like my entire lifetime. It was they who provided the emotional succour that I needed. My life with them was rather austere, but I did not regret what I had done even for a moment.

Was it a cloistered life?

It was a life dedicated to learning. I did not learn through formal training alone, but also by accompanying my gurus to recitals night after night, either theirs or someone else's, discussing the nuances of each the next morning. For me, my gurus represented the trinity of Brahma–Vishnu–Mahesh. As Brahma, the creator, the guru or potter takes a lump of clay and softens it with water. Then as Vishnu, the protector, he kneads it and gives it a shape. Finally, as Maheshwara, the revealer, he bakes the pot in the furnace and makes it perfect for receiving knowledge. The teachings of my gurus resonate in a powerfully personal way even today. And it was not always about dance alone. I had my moments of fun.

Allowing life's little dramas and adventures to creep in once in a while, Sonal laughs at the recollection of sharing a gin and lime with her gurus—her very first—and the long, intense conversations in the course of the occasional wine-and-gin-fuelled dinners at home.

What about random experiments, pointless digressions, that are part of being young?

No, my preoccupations were far from being typically adolescent. I created a sort of mental scaffolding to keep away temptations. My body, soul, expressions, moods, ideas and thoughts—all moved around dance. Professor Rao was an exacting teacher and the practice sessions were hard work.

* * *

Sonal continued to learn, performing occasionally at prestigious festivals. Back in Bombay, she danced on the occasion of the inauguration of a school of the Dagar brothers, sharing the platform with Ustad Vilayat Khan at the Tejpal Auditorium near Gowalia Tank. She danced at the Hasman Theatre of the Bhulabhai Institute, where she was invited to perform by the Asian Arts and Culture Centre. The dance critic of the *Indian Express* commented on her expressive eyes that portrayed expressions or bhavas in all their shades, and on her abhinaya which was seen at its best in the rendering of Jayadeva's *ashtapadis*.[30] He also commented on many unusual and new adavus that were blended with the ones commonly used in the Pandanallur style and the rhythmic patterns in the varnam which were striking and original. Reporting about the same event, the dance critic of the *Times of India* wrote, 'It was a discerning audience and the impressions that Sonal made on it was not only instant but profound. She has the makings of a first-rate dancer.' Then there were some critics who seemed content to fetishize her loveliness.

Sonal also began giving lecture-demonstrations. Her first lec-dem was at the campus of the United States Information Service in Bombay in 1962 to a select Indian-American audience. Her college friends were there; so were eminent artists like Ritha Devi, abstract painter Vasudeo Gaitonde, poet Pradyumna Tanna, and painter and art critic Gulam Mohammed Sheikh. She was the cynosure of all eyes.

> I remember dancing to a lullaby from *Krishna Karnamrita Slokam*.[31] Yashoda is putting little Krishna to sleep. He doesn't sleep, so she begins to tell him the story of Ram. When it comes to the point where Ravan has taken away Sita—at this point Krishna leaps out of his mother's lap shouting, 'Soumitri Lakshman, where is my bow?' I tried to bring out the element of wonderment when Krishna slips into Ram avatar or incarnation. I danced to a varnam in Raga Kamas and to demanding jathis. It was a feat of endurance and emotional intensity.

The audience erupted with open emotional admiration and Sonal remembers her ecstasy on waking up the next morning to discover that Ritha Devi had given her a glowing review in the *Times of India*. Her recital at a function organized by the Alliance Francaise also resulted in rave reviews. Her abhinaya was winsome, delicately shaded and delightfully uninhibited, especially in the portrayal of a lovelorn young woman.[32]

Sonal spent immersive days travelling to remote places to perform. She performed in small district towns and villages of Karnataka, travelling in bullock carts equipped with lanterns. She remembers performing in villages at the foothills of Mullayanagiri Range in the Chikkamagaluru district, at Doddaballapura, in spaces lit by petromax lights in front of entrancing, historic temples at Badami, Aihole, Pattadakal, Halebid and Hampi.

I was chewed alive by mosquitoes, the air heavy with humidity, but magical nonetheless, in the company of my gurus, under starlit skies surrounded by lush green plantations.

Some of these forays were part of the lec-dems organized by the Raos.

The novelty and excitement of dancing at the most unbelievable places still makes me smile. One of the most quirky memories is of the cattle fair at Badami. I was trying to touch up my face by the light of two petromax lamps before a recital when I heard drum beats and the hoarse voice of a man making an announcement in Kannada. Our vocalist Anoor Suri looked at me with twinkling eyes and said, 'You will dance to huge crowds today.' I asked, 'Why?' 'Well, this announcement is about the arrival of the most famous dancer from Bombay.' It took me a while to realize that the dancer was me!

Her performances with her gurus ended in 1962. She began to dance alone with musicians trained by Professor Rao. Her training in Bharatanatyam saw another phase in 1968–69, when she went to Madras to learn abhinaya from one of its greatest exponents, the legendary Mylapore guru, Gowri Ammal, who had taught both Rukmini Devi and Balasaraswati. Sonal travelled to her remote village by train, bus and bullock cart.

I was probably one of the last students on whom she spent so much time. She had a unique pedagogical style. There was no question of her teaching abhinaya gesture by gesture. She would repeat her performance over and over again, creating layers of meaning through her exquisite abhinaya. It was up to me to observe, imbibe and extrapolate. She taught padams replete with sringara bhava without even moving an extra inch of her supple hands, with intense expressions emanating from her one good eye. Her toothless smile would come out in a rare moment of appreciation when she liked what I was doing or even if one of her nuances eluded me.

During her stay in Madras, Sonal took classes in Kuchipudi from Dr Vempati Chinna Satyam at his Kuchipudi Art Academy, to understand the karanas of *Natyashastra* and their practice in the three contiguous dance styles from Orissa, Andhra and Tamil Nadu. She turned for her theoretical knowledge of the *Natyashastra* to Dr T.N. Ramachandran, an art historian and Sanskrit scholar considered the last word on the study and exposition of performing arts. She also continued with her Carnatic music lessons, learning the cherished compositions of the trinity of Carnatic singer–saint–composers, Tyagaraja, Shyama Shastri and Muthuswami Dikshitar, contemporaries of Beethoven.

* * *

You said somewhere that you dance for the joy of dancing, for the aesthetic pleasure, for the inner calm and peace that comes with dancing. What makes for a great classical dancer?

A celebrated critic wrote in the 1960s that if a dancer could go through the paces of the margam without violating the rules of rhythm and if this could be integrated with abhinaya, a dancer would make it to the renowned category—yet think of the number of dancers who bottomed out, drifted into obscurity.

Bharatanatyam is all about *nritta*, *nritya* and *natya*. *Nritta* is non-narrative and abstract dancing in which rhythm and the tala-cycle play a central role. The preparatory adavus, alarippu and *jatiswaram*, that follow belong to this element. *Nritya* is the poetic form of expressional dance, whereas *natya* is dramatic, theatre-like.

Finally, and overarchingly, there is a metaphysical dimension that only a few dancers are able to move towards and comprehend. When this happens, dance becomes *drishya-kavya* or visual poetry, and the dancer poet a great dancer. For instance, when I went to the Music Academy to watch a performance by Balasaraswati, her abhinaya took me to transcendental levels. She was dancing to her immortal, signature piece, *Krishna nee begane baro*, calling out to Krishna, beckoning to him by heaving her eyes and eyebrows, turning her shoulder and arms. Her bhavas and expressions were so real that I was convinced that my beloved godchild, with his little anklets and blue-sapphire bracelets, was somewhere close to her. My eyes too searched for him.

So the bhakti rasa[33] was clearly not only a dancer-centred experience but also immersed the audience.

Yes, it was an overwhelming aesthetic experience that enveloped everybody present there.

Balasaraswati's textual understanding of Bharatanatyam was also incredible, wasn't it?

Yes, even though she was essentially drawing from the textual authority of the *Natyashastra,* look how beautifully she deconstructed the margam, the linear format that all Bharatanatyam dancers must follow, drawing parallels between dance, temple architecture and ritual practice.

Let me read from her famous address to the Tamil Isai Sangam:[34]

> We enter through the *gopuram*[35] of *alarippu,*[36] cross the *ardhamandapam*[37] of *jatiswaram,*[38] the *mandapa*[39] of *sabdam*[40] and enter the holy precinct of the deity in the varnam. This is the place, the space, which gives the dancer expansive scope to revel in the rhythm, moods and music of the dance. The varnam is the continuum which gives ever-expanding room to the dancer to delight in her self-fulfilment by providing the fullest scope to her own creativity as well as to the tradition of the art.
>
> The padams follow. In dancing to the padams, one experiences the containment, cool and quiet of entering the sanctum from its external precinct. The expanse and brilliance of outer corridors disappear in the dark inner sanctum, and the rhythmic virtuosities of the varnam yield to the soul-stirring music and abhinaya of the padam. Dancing to the padam is akin to the juncture when the cascading lights of worship are withdrawn and the drum beats die down to the simple and solemn

chanting of sacred verses in the closeness of God. Then the tillana breaks into movement like the final burning of camphor.

Amazing poetic imagination. It is this quality, then, that makes a great dancer.

The repertory of a Bharatanatyam recital must have changed through the years.

Oh yes, even though largely dancers do not disturb the prescribed linear margam, they do dance to new sabdams, varnams, padams not presented earlier, amalgamating texts that were largely unexplored. A tillana too displays unusual patterns of choreography. But there has been a serious effort to revive old performing arts traditions by researching ancient Sanskrit texts, Tamil literature and temple sculptures.

Swapnasundari, for instance, has learnt the *Vilasini Natyam*[41] from surviving Andhra devadasis and has presented it in her performances.

What has changed irrevocably is the time spent on a performance. There was a time when a varnam alone lasted for more than two hours and the entire recital for four to five hours. I have sat through *Yakshagana*[42] performances with my gurus which would go on the whole night, beginning at ten and ending in the early hours of the next morning. Now even the most hard-core connoisseurs would not have that kind of time. A recital is usually wrapped up in two hours or even one.

You are a trained classical singer. One imagines that the chemistry between you and your musicians must have been extraordinary.

The alchemy that occurs between musicians and dancers is indeed extraordinary. The ragas to which varnams are set are tender, solemn ragas like Sankarabharanam, Todi, Nata Bhairavi, Kalyani, Karaharapriya, Kambodhi. These are ragas that lend themselves to elaborate delineations that are perfect for dance compositions.

When I dance, I interiorize the lyrics of the composition, the subtleties of the raga, expressing their nuances through my abhinaya. My musicians have been my anchors, my soulmates. What would my Bharatanatyam performances have been without Kamakshi Kuppuswamy's and Lalita Nagarajan's vocal renditions, Shivkumar's and K. Nagarajan's mridangam, Kausalya's veena, Sankaran's flute?

3

The Journey to Odissi

Sonal debuted in Delhi in 1964. Indrani Rahman, a leading Indian classical dancer, saw her perform in Bangalore, and charmed by her extraordinary talent, ensured that she was invited to perform at a prestigious festival at Sapru House in the heart of New Delhi. The festival, organized by the Indian Cultural Society, had an impressive line-up that included Kathak performances by maestros Damayanti Joshi and Roshan Kumari and a relatively new dancer, Bharati Gupta, a Kuchipudi performance by Indrani Rahman and sitar recital by Ustad Vilayat Khan. Economic historian Dr Dharma Kumar, parliamentarian and scholar Pandit Hriday Nath Kunzru, art scholar and historian Dr Kapila Vatsyayan, and Hungarian scholar and art critic Dr Charles Fabri were part of the audience on the evening of Sonal's performance on 9 October.

A little nervous about her debut, Sonal started with a rare alarippu in a thirteen-beat time cycle followed by jatiswaram, sabdam, varnam, padam, in the margam or the full repertory tradition of Bharatanatyam.[1] She ended her recital with tillana,

41

her sculptural body in perfect synchrony with rhythm and melody. For everyone present, there was no other place they would rather have been that evening. Her performance blew their mind. An avalanche of applause followed. Writing to her grandfather about the audience's response, Pandit Kunzru remarked, 'The audience cheered her after every dance and it was clear that the appreciation was not of the conventional kind but was genuine because everybody cheered her.' Sonal recalls being paid a small honorarium of Rs 450 for the performance.[2]

The acclaimed photojournalist Kishor Parekh, who revolutionized Indian reportage photography, was present at the recital that evening with his Nikon camera. His visual musings resulted in stunning, immaculately crafted photographs that were splashed in leading newspapers the next morning. Sonal was the hot new debutante of the season, almost a pin-up sensation. Writing for the *Statesman,* Charles Fabri described Sonal as a dancer of exquisite grace, with remarkable liquidity and spontaneity of movement. Another columnist and features editor covering the event for the *Indian Express* wrote that although this was her first performance in the capital, she had the making of a great dancer. 'She has an excellent style and performed the rhythmic sequences with verve, precision and a sense of line and proportion.'[3]

The evening was momentous in more ways than one. Sitting next to Charles Fabri in the first row was a dapper, young, foreign service probationer, Lalit Mansingh, who was clearly mesmerized. He accompanied Dr Fabri to the green room to congratulate Sonal once the performance was over, and managed to extract a promise to meet her the next day. Sitting in the back row were two other young men, Mani Shankar Aiyar, also a foreign service probationer, and Narendra Singh Bhati, a young Stephenian from the Jodhpur royal family. The former would rue laughingly, 'If I had been sitting in the front row, I would have got you, Sonal', and the latter would reappear in her life many years later, as a friend and lover.

Stories nest within stories in what followed over the next few days. Unsettled by the stirrings of love, Lalit started wooing Sonal who had stayed back in Delhi for a few days to learn padams from Swarnasaraswati, a cousin of the legendary Balasaraswati. Their meetings had some drippy, romantic moments but were far from being passionate and tempestuous. Sonal rationed out the time spent dating Lalit.

I was doing what Ondaatje[4] summed up in a similar context as the artist following the brush. I was excited at the possibility of learning new padams and put myself through an exacting daily regime of practice. So in a sense it wasn't a classic coup de foudre, but we walked through the quiet, languid streets of central Delhi, talking, laughing, sat on the sweet-smelling grass at India Gate eating ice creams, took an autorickshaw to Bengali Market to eat golgappas. Normal things, but by the time he left, there was something between us. Call it young love. Call it infatuation.

Certainly, there was something vital and unforgettable about the time spent in Delhi. Sonal returned to Bangalore. Lalit continued his probation in Delhi. They exchanged steamy letters reinforcing in her the conviction that they were meant to be together. There was an interlude of eight months before they met again. This time, it was in Bombay during Sonal's

Bharatanatyam recital at the Rabindra Natya Gruha, a cultural Mecca close to the Siddhivinayak temple. Sonal danced in the presence of her guru, Professor Rao, who conducted the recital. Her irresistible, heart-stoppingly beautiful performance kept the audience enraptured. Lalit too was completely bowled over.

They met at the Pakvasa residence later that night. It was Lalit's first encounter with Sonal's grandfather and parents during an excruciatingly formal family dinner. Among Sonal's candid anecdotes is an account of their response to her beau. Her grandfather and father seemed to like the reticent, handsome, urbane, young man. It did not take them long to warm up to him, but for her mother, Sonal's relationship with Lalit was a potential tinderbox of conflict. Cut up with Sonal for walking out of an arranged betrothal to a suitable suitor some time ago, she was at her sullen and wary best—like a mother-in-law in a tawdry, melodramatic sitcom.

> I remember her stiff upper lip, her hauteur. She seemed to recoil from the idea of his being an Oriya. Despite his being spectacularly eligible, he was clearly not her idea of a good suitor.

Sonal sneaked out at the crack of dawn the next morning to say goodbye to Lalit. Posted to Geneva, he was set to sail to Genoa in Italy, from where he was booked on a train to Geneva. Slender and petite, in her braided hair and a simple saree, Sonal was chaperoned by Shanta Bai, a family retainer. It was a sweet, very 1960s moment, lively and flirtatious, during which Lalit managed to discuss marriage. There were unspoken avowals of love. And when it was time for her to leave, he planted a little butterfly kiss on her cheek. The kiss that could not have lasted more than a millisecond removed all her doubts. Swept off her feet, Sonal was ready to be Lalit's wife.

Sonal's decision to marry Lalit felt like a leap of faith. A few trippy, uncertain days followed, but soon a registered envelope brought a formal wedding proposal from Lalit's father. Sonal's obduracy infused her parent's decision with a sense of urgency.

My parents felt that we were rushing into a lifelong commitment without knowing each other. But what I felt within me was something deep and strong. They had to eventually relent.

Sonal's father agreed to take her to Cuttack, a city in the eastern Indian state of Orissa, where Lalit's family lived, for a traditional Oriya betrothal ceremony. The father–daughter duo trawled through a map to trace the dots of their travel plans. A bumpy flight to Calcutta followed by a train ride brought them to Cuttack at the crack of dawn on a warm summer morning in April 1965. The telegram about their arrival plans somehow failed to reach Lalit's family. There was no one at the Cuttack station to receive them. They hired two rickshaws, one for their luggage and the other for themselves, and after moving through a labyrinth of narrow lanes and kuccha (unpaved) roads and losing their way many times, arrived at the Mansingh residence. In the early morning light, they looked as if they had stepped out of a regal Raja Ravi Varma[5] painting—Sonal in a beautifully draped cotton saree, her father in an achkan with silver buttons. Lalit's father, Dr Mayadhar Mansingh, opened the door, completely unprepared to see them at that unexpected hour. Overcoming his surprise, he welcomed them warmly, his handsome face creasing into a big, radiant smile.

The *nirbandha* or betrothal ceremony took place in a house teeming with relatives. While Dr Mansingh and Sonal's father took a ritual vow to get Sonal and Lalit married to each other, all Sonal remembers of the ceremony is a little exchange with her mother-in-law. 'You must have children,' said the matriarch fixing her with a gimlet eye. 'And they must speak Oriya,' was her next commandment. Sonal's response was quick and sharp. 'No, they will speak both Gujarati and Oriya,' she retorted, ignoring her mother-in-law's giant eye-roll.

Drawn to the ordinariness of Lalit's home but a little awkward initially, Sonal prepared herself for some amount of existential dissonance or revelatory close-ups that could be unsettling, but Lalit's father and siblings, brother Labanyendu, sisters Nivedita and Sanghamitra, were exceptionally warm. Their intimate conversations and playful bonhomie gave her a sense of belonging. Sexy, lively, even a little audacious, Sonal in turn wowed everyone. Reassured by what he saw, her father went back to Bombay. Sonal stayed back for two weeks at Dr Mansingh's request.

The time spent in Cuttack was to change the course of her life as a dancer. She developed a special closeness to Dr Mansingh, spending hours in his book-lined study-cum-bedroom trying to understand his artistic and literary sensibility. She was captivated by his intellectual heft and charisma. A leading educationist, credited with introducing the works of Shakespeare in Oriya literature, he was also known as *Premika Kabi* or a romantic poet. His first collection of poems,

Dhoop, had made him a household name. Many of his poems were set to music and were part of the Odissi dance repertory.

There was another facet of Dr Mansingh that has gone largely unreported. He was part of the post-1950s collective, a group of renowned Odissi gurus like Kalicharan Patnaik, Mahadev Rout, Raghu Datta, Pankaj Charan Das, Debaprasad Das, Kelucharan Mohapatra and Mayadhar Raut, that was trying to engage with the tumultuous history of Odissi and the movement to rebuild it from its vestigial remnants.

In the early 1950s, the Odissi repertory was really limited. When the first performance of Odissi was organized in Cuttack in 1953, it was based on a single composition of less than fifteen minutes. The reconstruction or revival involved study of ancient literary texts, and the dance movements reflected in bas-relief in historic temples of Parasurameswara, Brahmeswara and Konark. Starting from some of the earliest temples of the sixth century, there was barely a temple in Orissa where dance was not depicted in sculpture. The Utkal Nrutya Sangeet Natya Kala Parishad that was later converted into the State Sangeet Natak Akademi provided the much-needed official support for research and development of Odissi dance.

The recognition of Odissi as a classical dance form came in 1958. Described as the 'Odra-Magadhi' style of dance in the *Natyashastra,* sculptural evidence seems to indicate that Odissi was perhaps the oldest surviving dance form in India.[6] Over the centuries, three distinct styles of the dance emerged. The *mahari* tradition that flourished in temples is attributed to King Chodaganga Dev who built the Jagannath temple in Puri.[7] It ended with the recent death of Shashimani, the last living mahari at the temple. Married to the deity when she was barely seven, she danced inside the sanctum sanctorum morning and night to the lyrics of Jayadeva's ashtapadis. However, with the exception of Pankaj Charan Das, none of the other eminent Odissi gurus owed the genesis of their dance-acculturation to the mahari tradition.

The *nartaki* tradition of somewhat lascivious dance forms developed in the royal courts. It was at the centre of the anti-nautch movement in the early years of the twentieth century.

The *gotipua* tradition, represented by pre-pubescent boys in akharas[8] who were trained to dance, successfully weathered the anti-nautch blizzard. Dressed and made-up like girls, young boys danced outside temples to devotional poems of Vaishnava poets using simple footwork and acrobatic and tantric yogasanas. Even while being a male dance, gotipua was not completely testosterone-driven and included *lasya* or feminine movements. This tradition remained part of the Odissi DNA. Most Odissi gurus were trained gotipua dancers who were trying to walk the fine line between classical and neo-classical dance. Laxmipriya Mohapatra, wife of Sonal's guru, was the first woman to perform Odissi on stage, ending the traditional male hegemony over the dance form.

Overriding his wife's protests, Dr Mansingh wasted no time in taking Sonal to the Kala Bikash Kendra, an Odissi dance school started by Babulal Doshi in 1952, where Odissi guru Kelucharan Mohapatra was a revered teacher, with disciples of the stature of Sanjukta Panigrahi, Kumkum Das and Meenakshi Nanda. Sonal recalls that precious moment.

Dr Mansingh took me to Guruji and ordered, '*Ai Kelu, ayee mor bau Sonal, tame taku naach sikhaibo.*' ('Kelu, this is my daughter-in-law Sonal, you will teach her dance.') And that's how my journey in Odissi began.

Sonal put her learning process on a fast track in Cuttack. It was a riveting, adrenaline-packed period of her life. Travelling to the Kendra in a rickshaw every morning, she lost no time in embracing Odissi's melodic, lyrical form.[9] Using her body as the perfect instrument, she learnt to use the upper torso as an independent unit, gliding it from side to side. Combined with the frequent use of the triple-bent, asymmetrical tribhanga[10] posture involving deflections of the head, torso and hips, and gentle neck movements, Sonal epitomized the fluid grace that defines this classical form. Her hair brushed away from her face into a knot adorned by a flower-embedded headpiece representing the lotus, decked in traditional filigree silver jewels, she was ready to take her place as one of the outstanding legends of Odissi dance.

> Applying the body discipline and body intelligence of Bharatanatyam, I practised long hours perfecting the tribhanga and *chowka* (the squatting posture), the basic postures on which the entire technique of Odissi rests—all within the short span of fifteen days. Odissi's permanent mood or *sthayibhava* is essentially sringara, and I lost no time in embracing that.

In between her practice sessions, she allowed herself unfettered, pleasurable moments talking to Nivedita, fondly nicknamed 'Kuni', or teasing Sanghamitra, the baby of the family. She remained under the tutelage of Kelucharan Mohapatra for nearly seven years, but also took the best from other illustrious Odissi gurus like Mayadhar Raut and Srinath Rout.

A couple of years later, Sonal met Jiwan Pani, a poet, musicologist and distinguished scholar of Indian aesthetics and performing arts, one of the brightest of his generation. Their collaboration produced some of the most spectacular dance choreographies. Humane and generous, Jiwan Pani introduced Sonal to a range of performing art traditions of Orissa, like *Paala*, *Chhau*, *Chariya Geeti* and *Prahlad Natak*, a summation of years of research. Fired by his scholarly insights, Sonal's imagination was at its freest and most ambitious.

Reminiscing about his first encounter with Sonal in Puri, Jiwan Pani wrote:

It was a quiet but pleasant summer afternoon in 1967, and I was deeply engrossed in the poems of Elizabeth Jennings when I heard a soft tap on the door. Opening the door, to my great delight, I found Mayadhar Mansingh, the noted Oriya poet, standing before me. As I used to write poems in Oriya, he was for me almost a father figure. Behind him stood a radiant girl with large smiling eyes. She offered me a very sincere namaskar; I returned it with equal warmth. Mayadhar Mansingh introduced her to me saying, 'She is Sonal, my daughter-in-law.' When we settled down to tea, Mayadhar Mansingh said, 'Sonal in now learning Odissi from Kelu Babu. She has earlier learnt Bharatanatyam from Bangalore-based Professor Krishna Rao and Chandrabhaga Devi. Though she is perfecting her Odissi dance techniques under the guidance of Kelu Babu, she wanted to know about the aesthetics of Odissi dance and I thought you would be the right person to tell her, which is why we are here.' I felt flattered that Mayadhar Mansingh should choose me to explain to Sonal the aesthetics of Odissi. I was also deeply moved by his humility, considering that he was himself eminently qualified to speak, in great detail, on the subject. She had already perfected the basics of Odissi and was learning from her guru different dance items/numbers to expand her personal repertory.[11]

Beginning the early years of the 1970s, Sonal began composing at a feverish pace, building on Odissi's legacy but shaping it in a different way. To begin with, she focused on *mangalacharan*, the invocational item traditionally dedicated to the elephant-headed god, Ganesha, remover of obstacles. Sonal composed *Krishnashtakam*, based on a *stotra* (hymn) by Adi Shankaracharya;[12] *Jagannath Ashtakam*, based on a stotra by Chaitanya;[13] *Sankatmochan Hanuman Ashtakam* by Tulsidas;[14] parts of Devi stotras of Adi Shankara; Dasha Mahavidya hymns from *Devi Bhagavata Purana*[15] and *Shiva Tandava* of Acharya Abhinavgupta, a scholar of Shaiva philosophy.[16] She used the *Agni Suktam*, the first hymn in the Rig Veda, written by Rishika Vagambhrina,[17] to dance to the Devi as the supreme, all-pervading presence— her expressive style brilliantly nuancing the *sukta*: 'I transcend the heaven and yonder, the earth below and all the worlds. I, in my mighty grandeur, hold together all existence.'

Sonal was moving from creation to creation. There were several new compositions in *pallavi*, the pure dance imbued with nineteenth-century classicism. She reintroduced forgotten ragas, incorporated picturesque images of animals and birds for each note of their scales in dance movements, and reinvented a whole body of distinct movements to complement the musical compositions. She also forayed into the mystical realm of Vajrayana Buddhism that emerged in India in the sixth and seventh centuries. Drawing from the spiritual energy of this esoteric form, Sonal 'garnered priceless jewels' from *Chariya Geeti*, lyrical texts by some of the sixteen siddhas of this tradition written between the seventh and twelfth centuries.[18]

Old compositions were interleaved with innovative new nuances. For abhinaya, Sonal found herself delving into the richness of traditional Sanskrit texts, dealing with their narrative complexity with deftness. Songs of Oriya poets with their mythic, folkloric elements were already part of the Odissi repertory. She explored the incredible treasure of Oriya poetry written between the seventeenth and nineteenth centuries to include in her repertory several new, expressional pieces. Encouraged by Jiwan Pani, she used the ballad style singing of the Paala tradition[19] to compose expressional pieces, like *Sunayana*[20] and *Sukuntala*.[21] More than a dozen abhinaya pieces inspired by the songs of Meera,[22] Tulsidas and Surdas,[23] and contemporary poets like Kalicharan Patnaik, Jiwan Pani and Sitakant Mahapatra followed. Jayadeva's ashtapadis set to music by Bankim Sethi,[24] one of the most gifted of her generation of Odissi musicians, were also a precious part of her repertory.

* * *

What is it that turns abhinaya into such delicious mind candy?

Its ability to not only recreate reality but transform it through a range of evocative expressions. With a flick of her index finger, a dancer summons her errant lover to her presence. The same finger raised upwards above the head points to the supreme being. Placed near the dancer's temple and twisted around, it shows delusion, madness or forgetfulness. Hands are not alone in their quest for expression. The face, especially the eyes play an equally important role, sometimes even rendering the use of hand gestures unnecessary. They summon, reject, yearn, mock and beseech, creating moments of astonishing beauty, of lingering eroticism.

The aesthetics of movement and abhinaya has been summed up beautifully in an ancient Sanskrit verse that I love quoting to my students:

Yato hastastato drishti
Yato drishtistato manaha
Yato manahastato bhava
Yato bhavastato rasa.
Where the hand goes, the eyes follow
Where the eyes move, the mind follows
Where the mind is, emotions arise
Where emotions ripple, rasa permeates the work of art.

My abhinaya guru Gowri Ammal typified this. Towards the later part of her life, she almost lost her vision. Despite her failing health, she was always in an ecstatic state while teaching padams and *javalis*[25] depicting several moods of a woman in love—a state of absolute bliss, or *brahmananda,* where the finite and infinite merge.

The concept of rasa is seminal to the aesthetics of classical Indian dances, isn't it?

The 'Rasadhyaya' of the *Natyashastra* clearly says that no meaningful idea is conveyed if rasa is not evoked. Hence, the understanding of rasa is central to Indian classical dance aesthetics. The rasas rising from corresponding sthayibhavas or pervading stable emotions have been classified under eight categories. *Sringara*, or love, is the *adi* or primary emotion, followed by *hasya* (mirth), *karuna* (pathos or compassion), *raudra* (fierce), *vira* (valour), *bhaya* (fear), *vibhatsa* (repugnant) and *adbhuta* (wondrous).

The ninth rasa is *shanta* (serene), which was made part of the cosmos of rasas in the eleventh century. Together the *navarasa*s coexist, merge, or even metamorphose, to represent a varied, rich range of emotions and aesthetic experiences for both the artist-creator and the spectator. In addition, there are thirty-three transient bhavas, or emotive states, known as *vyabhichari* that are evoked to nuance the nine dominant ones to create the composite experience of *rasanubhava* (experience of rasa), *rasabhivyakti* (expression of rasa) and *rasautpati* (evocation of rasa).

In Odissi, as in Bharatanatyam, you have explored the fault line between classicism and innovation. Is classicism and continuity more important to the dance technique and repertory, or innovation?

I think we place unreasonable emphasis on purity and classicism. Predictability is the death of art. Moreover, it is a bit strange to use the concept of purity for forms that have evolved over thousands of years. Even while she valorized tradition, if Balasaraswati performed the same composition at two different places, you could be sure that each of the two versions would be different in terms of improvisations.

Classicism certainly does not preclude creative improvisations, neither does originality distort tradition. A genre that remains unchanging and has nothing new to offer can only be stultifying and boring. However, the basic syntax and the core which is a collective memory, either in the form of *shruti*, that which is heard, or in the form of *smruti*, that which is remembered, endures the vicissitudes of time, and is relevant even today. It is also a question of what works where. For instance, if innovative modern and postmodern choreographies work in North America and Europe, traditional aesthetics works best in diasporic South Asian communities.

Some of the most spectacular music is dance music.

Indeed. In the repertory of Odissi, for instance, a pallavi is always named after a raga and is a visual interpretation of the melodic movement of a given raga, the cadences of which go on looping through one's mind long after a performance is over. Odissi music has developed as an exquisite counterpoint to the Hindustani and Carnatic classical music traditions, with its own distinct ragas, talas and style of rendition.

When I performed, it was mostly Bankim Sethi who took care of my Odissi vocals accompanied by an accomplished ensemble of musicians playing the *mardala* (of which the pakhawaj is a variant), flute, *gini* (*manjeera*, small cymbals), tanpura (drone), sarod or the sitar. Sometimes, I even used two voices in the same alliterative mode.

If you had to choose, what would it be—Bharatanatyam or Odissi?

You are making it sound like Sophie's Choice (*laughs*). I share an equal passion for Bharatanatyam and Odissi. Bharatanatyam is majestic, geometrical in conception, architectural, whereas Odissi is lyrical, graceful and sculptural. Very alluringly, together they create a unified vision of aesthetics.

Did Cuttack work its spell on you?

Yes. The city had a subtle charm. More importantly, its relationship with Odissi and related dance forms was organic and visceral. I cruised through its potholed roads to see cultural events. Tradition echoed along its streets. I managed to see several gotipua performances in the precincts of old temples. I saw the maharis dance while on a boat ride (*chaapa*). Cuttack is also associated with memories of my father-in-law, an extraordinary person whom I loved deeply.

4

In Geneva

Betrothed to Lalit, Sonal arrived in Geneva in the last week of July 1965, a little dewy-eyed, a little in love, to keep her date with her wedding. Accompanying her were her father and sister. Lalit was at the airport with an armful of asters and carnations, his eyes moist with tenderness. A short taxi ride in the neon sunshine took them to Lalit's transit accommodation at Quai Gustave-Ador, facing the crescent-shaped lake, Lake Geneva (Lac Leman) and the Jet d'Eau fountain. Geneva's postcard-perfect charm instantly captivated Sonal.

She, in a sense, planned her own wedding, down to every bridezilla detail, traipsing around the old city's cobblestone alleys with her sister. She wore a red silk Oriya *ikat* saree for a civil ceremony at the Mayorie, the civil registrar's office, that was followed by a Hindu wedding on the third of August. Sonal was stunning in her red-and-white traditional Gujarati wedding saree (*panetar*), and Lalit handsome in a traditional silk dhoti–kurta ensemble. A retired UN diplomat, Dr Raghunath Rao, doubled up as the priest, chanting Vedic shlokas on a pleasant autumnal evening on the terrace of the consul general's apartment block. Stripped to its bare essentials, the brief ceremony was followed by a reception where she stunned again, her face aglow in a fiery red temple saree embellished with gold brocade.

Sonal slipped into her new life with a little trepidation. Her acquaintance with Lalit had been somewhat fleeting. She was charmed by him, intrigued by his intellect, his artistic and literary taste, but did not know what to expect from her marriage. Her anxiety was short-lived. Exulting in her extraordinary beauty and luscious sensuality, Lalit engulfed her with a tenderness and passion she had never experienced before. They were lovers almost immediately, her passion matching his. Their warm new apartment at 4, Rue De-Beaumont, close to the Museum of Art and History, had large windows fringed with honeysuckle creepers and lavender shrubs. She found in their vivid colours and fragrance a metaphor for her new life.

'A single metaphor can give birth to love,' wrote Milan Kundera in *The Unbearable Lightness of Being*. Sonal found her first young love in Lalit, and also in the banal, daily rhythms of her life. Their love was no fauxmance. She remembers the achingly tender moments spent strolling quietly through the city's chic streets, their playful tongue-in-cheek banters on the *mouette*[1] on moonlit nights, their picnics on Mont Salève, letting down their guard while coping with their sense of loss after a sudden, unexpected miscarriage.

Sonal filled her apartment with art and oddities and quirky trinkets from India. It soon became one of the hottest spots for travelling artists passing through the city, attracting the likes of Ravi Shankar, M.S. Subbulakshmi and Ali Akbar Khan, all old family friends. Sonal remembers spending interesting, salon-like evenings with them and other friends, away from the razzmatazz of consulate events. 'Geneva is unusually lovely with sunshine every day, birds chirping, spring flowers blossoming . . .' she wrote in a letter to Arti, her sister, continuing to find an echo of her own joy in the city's loveliness. Arti visited a couple of times with her husband Dhananjay and son Divyang, a blue baby getting treated in a hospital in Houston. Sonal looked forward to these visits, connecting with her sister and the young child with a quiet but deep affection.

Starting as a complete novice, over a few months, Sonal learnt to fork out delicious meals in her airy, spacious kitchen— rice and lentils, fish steamed with olives and oregano, spaghetti with clams, chicken roasted in wine, Caesar salad with parmesan flakes teamed with sherry or port.

My life swerved off its expected course. I reconfigured it around Lalit's needs. I was the quintessential good wife and hostess. I chopped, cleaned, baked, expanded my cooking repertory to include meat and fish even though I continued to be a strict vegetarian. I dutifully attended parties at the consulate.

However, even though a part of her craved to be the most banal of women, the most prosaic, and ready to revel in nondescript moments, her life in Geneva did not flatten into the prototype of a foreign service wife's life hemmed in by official protocol.

Contrary to her initial expectations, her days were awash with tides of creativity. A debut recital at the consulate within weeks of her arrival in Geneva was followed by a performance at the Musée et Institut d'ethnographie.² The Indian Association of Geneva, in collaboration with Air India and Indo-Swiss Society, invited her to perform at the Hotel Intercontinental in Geneva. Her incredible talent and charisma drew immediate attention. Her dance grew wings. A letter written by Sean P. Kennan, the permanent representative of Ireland to the European office of the United Nations, to his Indian counterpart, M.K.P. Lukose, is indicative of the buzz created by Sonal's performances:

> My wife and I wish to thank Mrs Lukose and you most sincerely for having given us the privilege of watching the superb performance of Indian Dancing by Mrs Mansingh, at your Mission, last night.
>
> This was indeed, a fine cultural treat of the highest artistic quality and I should like to say that we enjoyed the whole evening immensely.

She was invited for lec-dems in Berne, Basel and Zurich. She danced at the Ancient Theatre at Luxembourg a day after a performance by Ravi Shankar and Alla Rakha, receiving an equally deafening standing ovation. Writing to her sister on 9 March 1966, soon after another performance at Hotel Intercontinental organized by the Indian Association for about 800 people, Sonal gushed, 'People were in raptures and I got more ovation and notices than Ravi Shankar . . . Lalit is punching my head every day to keep it from swelling.'

Invited by the Deutsch-Indische Gesellschaft, the German–Indian Association, with Dr Klein at its helm, for a tour of Germany in 1967, she debuted on the studio stage of the Kieler

University at Wuppertal, dancing the full Bharatanatyam margam, following it up with Odissi and Kuchipudi in the second part of the performance. These two dance forms had not been seen in Germany until then. This was followed by a spate of recitals in other German towns and cities that included Hamburg, Frankfurt, Bremen, Hannover, Darmstadt, Stuttgart, Munich, Saarbrücken, and in the assembly hall of the Herzog-Ernst school in Uelzen. She also danced for the German television. After one such performance, a German newspaper reviewer wrote, 'Would the title of Miss Grace exist, Sonal Mansingh from India should get it. With just as much grace as had earned discipline, the twenty-two-year-old wife of the Indian consul in Geneva, is dancing into the hearts of the people.'[3]

For almost all her performances, Sonal travelled alone with her spool tapes and costumes, using the time spent on narrow-gauge railways to read or gaze at the vast stretches of green vineyards and wooded mountains.

I was very young, reasonably attractive, and full of enthusiasm about Germany, which in turn translated into a warm reception from the local people with whom I stayed during the tour.

She also toured and performed in Belgium,[4] France and the United Kingdom, giving altogether forty-two performances, taking the flurry of extraordinary attention focused on her in her stride.

One of the many experiences that Sonal enjoys sharing was being invited to dance at the Abbey St. Pierre at Ghent, where the vast refectory was full of international celebrities and diplomats. The occasion was the celebration of Indo-Belgian Friendship Week. She had stars in her eyes when she arrived for her performance.

Mani Shankar Aiyar, who was the second secretary, offered to run the tape recorder for me, compering in French and holding face tissues and a glass of lemon juice fortified with glucose to replenish my energy during the long recital. That evening, something possessed me. I abandoned myself to my dance, so much so that my nose ring decided to forsake me and danced right across the stage into the lap of K.B. Lall, the Indian ambassador.

Sonal enjoys sharing memories of her performances in the UK. Her gurus, the Raos, were there at the time, invited by the Asian Music Circle headed by Yehudi Menuhin to perform and teach Bharatanatyam to students in Cambridge and London. She performed with them at the Commonwealth Institute, followed by solo performances at the universities in Nottingham, Durham and Cambridge. Her solo recital in London was also a tour de force. Her extraordinary onstage appeal and her rendition—rich, expressive and brimming with beauty—created a genuine interest in Indian classical dances.

Sonal continued her gruelling practice sessions despite the constraint of not being able to use her apartment.

Initially, unmindful of the Swiss passion for peaceful surroundings, I thumped away in my first-floor apartment. My landlady put a stop to that. I still remember the startled expression on her face when she came up to see what was happening. 'You look so tiny, how do you manage to produce such earth-shattering sounds? My chandelier is swaying crazily and will break!' she exclaimed.

Sonal had to scout for an alternative space for her long hours of practice—dingy cellars, the basement of the Air India office, the villas of friends, whatever space was available at the consulate. She spent hours trudging through snow with her dance music tapes and practice costume. Geneva was where her first student, a seventeen-year-old Swiss–French girl, Anne Marie Francoise, appeared at her doorstep unexpectedly one morning, entranced by her persona and her dance. Sonal taught her and three other students, one of them the granddaughter of Max Petitpierre, a former president of the Swiss Confederation.

The two years that the Mansinghs spent in Geneva were momentous in many ways. It was an interesting period in Europe, defined by the revolutionary, anarchic, liberating strands of counterculture and the emergence of the 'New Left'. The Prague Spring followed in 1968, featured in several works of literature including Milan Kundera's 1984 postmodern novel, *The Unbearable Lightness of Being*. Sonal spent many evenings at the Opera House and the Grand Theatre de Geneve with Lalit, following a cycle of riveting performances, spoilt for choice. It was at the Opera House that she was transfixed by the visceral body language and incredible chemistry between Margot Fonteyn and Rudolf Nureyev when they danced together in a ballet called 'Marguerite and Armand', based on Alexandre Dumas's play, *La Dame aux Camélias* (*The Lady of the Camellias*).

* * *

You lived in Europe in the 1960s, a period known for its excesses, synonymous with new, radical, subversive events.

It was a wonderful time to be there—a period of radical political change. Thirty-two African countries were decolonized, restoring agency to their people. It was an era of protest, of anti-war marches. Europe was awakening not only to new forms of politics but also new forms of art, literature and music. There was unprecedented interest in Eastern mysticism, philosophy, culture, yoga and the arts. So much of the arts converged in Europe.

This was when many leading musicians turned to Indian music following The Beatles. Was it the same in dance?

There was certainly a buzz surrounding Indian dances. There were several performances organized in small, intimate spaces for a friendlier, less edgy audience. My audience, for instance, expected me to decode the semiotic lexicon of my dance, till then known as 'Hindoo' temple dance or oriental dance, its cultural history, even its genealogy before a performance. Their interest never ceased to amaze me. There was a genuine hunger and need for experiencing new art forms. I had to sometimes take eight curtain calls after my performance.

You saw a lot of auteur-style cinema.

Yes, I was bewitched by the art-house films of Fellini, Truffaut, Resnais, Buñuel, Ray and others. My mind was on seize!

What were you reading?

Fiction mostly.

I read from a towering pile of books drawn out of cartons from India. I also read some of the most original voices of the 1960s from Europe, America and Russia— John Updike, Harold Pinter, Anthony Burgess, Muriel Spark, Simone de Beauvoir and many others.

Were you also following fashion trends or did you continue to dress up like your mother, circa 1940?

This was a period when everything was being debunked. There was no single trend—if the boutiques and ateliers of Chanel and Yves Saint Laurent were the rage, so were the trends set by the hippies. I stuck to my own personal style evolved over years spent in Bombay and Mysore, dancing, and travelling through rural India.

This was a period when second-wave feminism grabbed eyeballs and important polemicists and theorcticians of feminism like Kate Millett challenged the fundamental assumptions of patriarchy. There was a stubborn, petulant misogyny even in a country like Switzerland that did not give women the right to vote until 1971. How much did feminism impact you?

I was focused on dance, but certainly a part of my own political ideology was peppered by feminism. I made choices that were feminist. My friends were people with sharp intellects and a deep understanding of art in Zurich, Basel, Geneva and Paris. They pre-empted answers to questions that dogged me at that point and opened me to the reawakening of Europe.

5

A-45, Pandara Road

When the Mansinghs returned to India, a buzz had already built around her. She danced at the Sur Sringar Samsad festival at the Rang Bhawan in Bombay on her return in August 1967, much before the latter was declared part of the silent zone, and a month later joined her husband to set up home temporarily at a transit accommodation on Curzon Road (now renamed Kasturba Gandhi Marg) and then on Pandara Road, a smart little bureaucratic enclave for young officers in the heart of Lutyens' Delhi.

Delhi at this point was a stimulating and exciting city churning with multitudes of new ideas and initiatives. One of the pioneering initiatives in the field of performing arts came before Independence, in 1936, when a leading cultural reformer, Nirmala Joshi,[1] started a school of music and dance with an incredible faculty of distinguished artists. Pushing aside the rather hegemonic control of the gharanas, she managed to persuade Achhan Maharaj[2] to teach Kathak to students who were outside the bloodline of his gharana. Amongst his foremost students was Sharan Rani, one of India's leading sarod players. Another notable alumnus was Kapila Vatsyayan, then known by her maiden name, Kapila Malik. Three years later, Vinay Chandra Maudgalya from the Gwalior gharana, a disciple of the veteran musician, Vinayakrao Patwardhan, founded the Gandharva Mahavidyalaya, an impressive music school, in a tiny little house in Connaught Place.

In the absence of well-equipped auditoriums, classical music performances were organized at the homes of patrons. The Curzon Road home of the industrialist Sir Shri Ram witnessed many interesting musical soirées. A night-long concert of classical music supported by Sumitra, his young daughter-in-law, became the most popular music event in the city's history. Known as the Shankarlal Festival,[3] it continues as an annual feature, hosting some of the biggest legends in classical music in the shabby cosiness of a large hall.

Sumitra Charat Ram started the Jhankar music circle around the same time. Jhankar was creatively nourished by maestros like Siddheshwari Devi, Hafiz Ali Khan, Baba Allauddin Khan, Shambhu Maharaj, Ravi Shankar, Birju Maharaj, Durga Lal and Aminuddin Dagar, and later grew into the Shriram Bharatiya Kala Kendra[4] in the Mandi House area, the cultural centre of the city.

Active government endowments and support resulted in the creation of several beautiful creative spaces for fine arts and performing arts in the 1950s, such as the Sangeet Natak Akademi, Lalit Kala Akademi, Sahitya Akademi, the National Gallery of Modern Art and the National School of Drama. Around the same time, buildings equipped with auditoriums, like Sapru House, Vigyan Bhawan, Rabindra Bhawan and the new building of the All India Fine Arts and Crafts Society came up, energizing the city's cultural spaces. Delhi was embraced by legends like Ali Akbar Khan, Ravi Shankar, Hafiz Ali Khan, Shambhu Maharaj, Siddheshwari Devi and many other artists who set up homes here.

Sonal was enthralled to be back to the city she had grown to love, and plunged into her chosen life unfettered. Her itinerary was packed with Bharatanatyam and Odissi recitals. She prefaced the recitals with dance commentaries and annotations—something that had not really been tried till then. She not only had her audience completely entranced, but also the dance critics. Reporting on her recital at Sapru House in October 1967, the *Hindustan Times'* critic wrote, 'This was Bharatanatyam with all its grace, beauty, gentleness and vigour.'[5] Another dance critic in *The Statesman*, after watching a performance organized by the Little Theatre Group at the same venue a few months later, wrote:

Sonal Mansingh is among the most outstanding exponents of Bharatanatyam endowed with both dignity and grace, and splendid in her facial expressiveness. She has lovely hand and finger movements, a most flexible face and a lightness in her 'elevations' that put her into the category of the best dancers of India.[6]

Commenting on the incredible visual bravura of Sonal's Odissi performance at the Mavalankar Auditorium, *Link* magazine's dance critic wrote:

Sonal's recital offered an illuminating glimpse into the sensuous and lyrical magnificence of this dance of antiquity from Orissa. In the rendering of ashtapadis and pallavis she touched sensual and lyrical heights. The wreath of beauty she placed on Jayadeva's lyrical compositions had a luxuriating poetic charm, broken now and then by the radiating glory of the sculpturesque poses.[7]

Also commenting on her languorous, irresistible Odissi oeuvre, art scholar and historian Mohan Khokar wrote:

Sonal's performance was full of several lovely pictorial moments and were at times marked by a pungency that was striking. Her hands and arms were throughout neat and delicately propulsive. Towards the end of the Bhairavi Pallavi she was able to work herself up to a tremendous cacophony of movement and pose and sound and rhythm, which had the sparkle of a many-faceted gem.[8]

And this is how it went in review after review as Sonal shaped the dance history of Bharatanatyam and Odissi.

In addition to these two dance forms, Bharatanatyam and Odissi, Sonal also occasionally performed Kuchipudi. Amongst her most notable performance was a recital at the historic Annapurna Theatre in Cuttack in May 1968, in the presence of her father-in-law and leading Oriya critics and connoisseurs. Covering this event for the *Amrita Bazar Patrika*, an art critic wrote, 'It was a dance performance of superb order and the Kuchipudi dance particularly drew applause from the audience. Her Odissi too was performed excellently in a most authentic way.'[9]

Interspersing her recitals with training, Sonal made several trips to Cuttack to continue her Odissi training with

Kelucharan Mohapatra. During his long teaching assignments in Delhi, she joined his classes at the Nritya Niketan set up by Harekrishna Behara[10] in a tiny flat at Bhagat Singh Market in Connaught Place and at Kumkum Mathur Lal's spacious residence at 4, Lytton Lane.[11] The Nritya Niketan attracted a distinguished visiting faculty. Sonal's learning process was enriched by interactions with Mayadhar Raut and young exponents of Odissi who attended classes there. This group included dancers like Kumkum Mathur, Yamini Krishnamurthy, Aloka Panikar, Rani Karna, Priya Pawar and Radha Reddy.

The group participated in several programmes together. This included a dance-drama called *Kanchi Vijaya*, based on a popular legend associated with Jagannath,[12] which was staged at the auditorium of AIFACS, the All India Fine Arts and Crafts Society. 'It was a stirring production,' reminisces Kumkum. 'Sonal was Princess Padmavati. She looked stunning, danced beautifully. Her rendering of *Dashavatara*, the story of Lord Vishnu's ten incarnations, was absolutely inimitable.'[13] Sonal remembers the production for an added reason.

Princess Padmavati was from Kanchipuram, hence the first part of my dance was based on Bharatanatyam. I wore an almond-coloured costume with a blue-and-gold border over my camouflaged golden yellow Odissi costume, which I had to wear for the Odissi *Dashavatara* rendition. I had exactly seven minutes to change. The green room could only be reached by running up a rather precarious spiral staircase. So I had just enough time to pull off my Bharatanatyam costume and rush for the next part of the dance-drama.

In another memorable evening of Odissi dance organized by Nritya Niketan at Sapru House, Sonal danced solo, while Kumkum and a couple of other young dancers performed in groups. Sonal's *Sringara Pallavi, Dashavatara* and *Phulwari Leela*,[14] exquisitely rendered, were feted by several critics and connoisseurs. 'Sonal Mansingh gave an evocative exposition of the Sringara Pallavi in Raga Saveri,[15] creating the appropriate rasa (mood) by gesture and expression. Her Dashavatara was notable for rhythmic footwork and excellent abhinaya. The Phulwari Leela of Tulsidas contained several passages of choreographic delight.'[16]

Sonal also regularly rehearsed at Triveni Kala Sangam, a creative space designed by the noted American architect, Joseph Allen Stein, and run by Sundari Shridharani, a student of Uday Shankar. A celebrity hangout, Triveni attracted artists, poets, musicians, sculptors, photographers and young students, and was reflective of a mix of cultures, both the high end and the Bohemian. Its open-air theatre, with state-of-the-art acoustics, hosted art, experimental cinema, classical dance and music events. Sonal walked to Triveni every afternoon during her stay at the Curzon Road hostel to rehearse to canned music. At the same time, she worked hard on being a good wife—driving her husband up the Raisina Hill every morning, ferrying him lunch, learning not to get impatient with the minutiae of life as a bureaucrat's wife—arranging dinners and attending receptions.

It was a momentous time in many ways. Sonal was invited for a number of Bharatanatyam and Odissi performances at prestigious *sabha*s in Madras. When she performed Odissi at the Museum Theatre under the joint auspices of the Bharatiya Vidya Bhawan, Kala Kendra and Max Mueller Bhawan, the intimate physical space of the theatre resonated with the repeated applause of a rapturous audience. Rukmini Devi, the cause célèbre of Indian dance, was present at the recital, as were M.S. Subbulakshmi, revered Bharatanatyam teacher Vazhuvoor Ramaiah Pillai, and Sanskrit scholar and musicologist V. Raghavan, among others.

Sonal, accompanied by her guru Kelucharan Mohapatra on the mardala,[17] performed to one of poet Jayadeva's most erotic ashtapadis from the *Geet Govind*.[18] The Sanskrit text of the ashtapadi reads, '*Kuru Yadunandana chandana shishira tarena karena payodhare*.' Addressed to Krishna, the translated version of this couplet draws poetic images of desire and erotic longing, 'Oh joy of the Yadav clan, with your hands that are cooler than sandalwood paste, please draw designs of tender leaves on my pitcher-like breasts.'[19] Its exposition in dance often lurched on risqué, and posed a challenge. On one occasion, Rukmini Devi had famously walked out of the performance of a well-known Odissi dancer, finding her embellished exposition of this ashtapadi overtly sexualized. Sonal managed to unfold the allegorical nuances of Jayadeva's poetry in a delicate play of yearning and passion. Her restrained, tender, expressive vocabulary, and her interplay of gaze and movements delighted her audience. Even Rukmini Devi was enraptured and stunned by her virtuosity. It was an evening of pure joy, and Sonal received dream reviews in local newspapers and tabloids.

Sonal's recital at the annual festival of the Music Academy, a leading arts institution in Madras, also received superlative reviews. A reputed art columnist commented,

Sonal Mansingh's Odissi was an essay in sophistication and lyricism both in presentation and performance. The postures were exquisite, traditional and very classical. The movements had elegance and were a visual delight. An intricate pallavi with elaborate cross-rhythm formulations and variations suggestive of the highbrow flavours of the Bharatanatyam varnam highlighted this recital in which Sonal's footwork, most artistically aligned to the rhythmic sequences vocalised and played on the mardala by her guru Kelucharan Mohapatra, was lovely to watch. Her expressiveness eloquently communicated the ashtapadi themes danced by her.[20]

Amongst the notable events of this phase of her life, Sonal remembers a memorable two-and-a-half-month-long dancing tour of the USSR, Mongolia, Poland and the erstwhile German Democratic Republic (East Germany) in 1968.

I danced in East Berlin, Halle, Dresden, Erfurt and Weimar. Weimar had a special place in my heart as it was here that Goethe's autobiographical novel, *Die Leiden des jungen Werthers* (*The Sorrows of Young Werther*), was set. The famous school of music named after Franz Liszt was our arena of action. I had a huge fan club of students and artists that followed me around to other cities too. A handsome young tenor lost his heart to me. When it was time for me to leave, he bid me a sad and passionate farewell in full view of the rather shocked Indian cultural delegation.

Poland evokes sad memories. It was in a small, austere hotel room, on 6 November 1968, when someone from the Indian embassy brought a telegram from Mohan Khokar informing

Sonal of her grandfather's death. She was devastated. She had lost her co-conspirator, mentor and enlightened soulmate. Her room turned into an incubator of memories as she tried to cope with the intensity of her emotions. A grand felicitation by the Communist Party Congress at Warsaw also did not stop her from agonizing for days about why she had not taken time off to meet him at the beginning of the long trip.

Sonal came back to India to enter another period of creative tailspin, giving one performance after another, each marking a high point in her oeuvre. A riveting trip with then prime minister Indira Gandhi as part of a cultural delegation to Afghanistan along with famous artists like Begum Akhtar, Pandit Ram Narayan and Damayanti Joshi followed, together with performances at prestigious festivals like the Berlin Festival and the Shiraz festival in Iran.

A two-month stay in Osaka, performing on an average three times a day to packed houses at the amphitheatre of the Indian Pavilion at Expo '70, brought her superlative acclaim from the local tabloids. A report captioned 'Exquisite Sensuous Beauty' in the *Mainichi Daily News* (1 July 1970) cryptically noted that 'the number of visitors to the Indian pavilion at Expo '70 has certainly increased notably because the most celebrated dancer of India is performing every day.'

> For me, representing Indian classical performing art was no picnic. The appearances were all too frequent and the rigours of the engagement a challenge to my power of endurance. I was truly spoilt by my audience. I remember an incident when the Crown Prince Akihito and Princess Michiko visited the pavilion to watch my performance.

While I was dancing, the Indian ambassador walked up and asked me to stop as the prince had to leave. The prince, however, was in no hurry to move. He sat through the entire recital and later asked probing questions about the hand and eye movements, the costume and the accessories.

It was not only Sonal's dance that was attracting attention. Young women would flock to her for beauty tips, fascinated by her kohl-lined eyes that seemed to give her a feline look. Many, to her amusement, asked her if her beautiful eyes and sharp nose were the result of surgical intervention. Expo '70 was memorable in other ways too. She took time off to listen to Stockhausen at the German Pavilion, who had been invited to present a five-and-a-half-hour live programme of his music every day for 183 days to an audience that rivalled hers. She also saw her first ever IMAX film, *Tiger Child,* at the Fuji group's pavilion, and was smitten by a large moon rock on display in the US pavilion that had been brought back by Apollo 12 astronauts in 1969. After the long stint in Osaka, Sonal and her troupe moved on to perform in other Southeast Asian countries.

Sonal's heart-wrenching beauty and personal style continued to draw outsized interest. Never really drawn to European haute couture, her wardrobe was a mix of contemporary chic and traditional, classical, handloom sarees. Fashion columnists trailed by photographers with polaroid cameras profiled her in her bright sarees, carefully taken out from their white paper cocoons, hair open or casually tied back, coiffed and styled only when she performed. The DNA of her style was also reflected in Thea Porter and Zandra Rhodes-inspired long skirts and kaftans draped around her hourglass frame.

During this time, her marriage too was under a lens. Sonal and Lalit Mansingh appeared to be the perfect, beautiful couple. Something, however, was beginning to change subtly and imperceptibly. Not yet past its sell-by date, their relationship was clearly moulding. The moments of physical intimacy were getting rarer. She could see him tune out and glaze over, no longer needing to warm up to her. And even though they tried to keep their personal issues away from probing eyes, there was already a whiff of scandal trailing her.

* * *

We are at a friend's café eating cheese toast with mushroom omelettes and hummus soaked in olive oil.

'What made you continue with him?' I ask, taking a sip from my bowl-sized cup of cappuccino.

My complacent naiveté? (*laughs*). On a more serious note, even though there was an underlying disquiet, a feeling that something was not quite right, the fact that my marriage was collapsing seemed outside the realm of the plausible. My friends tried to warn me about a bevy of young women in Lalit's life, but I continued to live in an anaesthetized haze, keeping myself insulated from the steamy details, managing somehow a Zen-like forbearance.

In a way, at this point, my life was a little surreal. On the one hand, dealing with a husband who was progressively getting as dry as a dry martini, on the other, the colourful spotlights, star-struck audience, pirouetting fans, and through all this, an incredible dance-driven adrenaline washing over me . . .

You were one of the most attractive, lusted-after women of the time.

In my case, the rumour mill has always been relentless. Even while it was Lalit who was playing around, it was I who was seen as a sexual temptress. My critics smelt promiscuity even when there was none. My only illicit pleasure was an occasional bar of Toblerone!

6

Scenes from a Marriage

In 1971, Lalit Mansingh moved to Kabul on a posting. Sonal followed him a little later. Already avant garde in the 1960s, Kabul reached an apotheosis in the early 1970s, evident from the photo stories of Mohammad Qayoumi and Farid Dastan.[1] Unravaged by war and terror, it was a gilded generation intoxicated by the possibilities of a truly liberal, westernized environment. Women had access to university education and professional lives of their choice. A woman Afghan model was featured on the cover page of *Vogue*. Sonal, already a celebrity, was welcomed warmly by flight attendants in their blue Ariana Afghan Airlines shirts and pencil skirts. They remembered reading about her in newspapers and tabloids during her last trip in 1969, when she was driven in an open limousine with Indira Gandhi through Kabul's central road, Idga Wat, to meet the fifty-five-year-old dapper king, Mohammad Zahir Shah. Some of them took her autograph.

The flight was delayed by five hours. I landed at Kabul to find Lalit missing. I was driven to the residence of his friends, Paul and Leela Mathiew, where a slightly drunk Lalit came to their garden gate to welcome me. Even though at that point I was dealing with a feeling of abandonment, of rejection, seeing the garden full of new faces, I managed a smile.

After spending a few weeks at the Kabul Hotel, the Mansinghs moved into an old, spacious, double-storeyed house with a stone stairway, near the Indian embassy. It was a house with grape arbours and a large, sun-cooked garden with cherry and apricot trees heavy with fruit. Thoroughly at ease in this new setting, Sonal turned the somewhat decrepit house into a warm home. Indian paintings were nailed to the walls, a huge kalamkari painting was draped along the staircase and exquisitely woven Afghan kilims covered the stone floors. She bought art from the local flea markets, and shopped in the centuries-old bazaars of Istalif for blue pottery, ceramics and affordable antiques.

Sonal resumed her dance practice, and shared her initial dance-related travails and agonies with Kumkum Mathur Lal: 'I started practice one morning and promptly broke the floor! The tiles have caved in, some are cracked and we had to have them cemented. So, here I am, contemplating dance in my mind, unable to thump and kick to my heart's content. Isn't it sad?'

For Sonal it was unthinkable to spend her days without dancing. In an attempt to keep her spirits up, she began accompanying Lalit on trips to the remotest and most extraordinary parts of the country, carrying a camera and a running supply of Kodachrome films. She spent time in the old city of Herat, at the crossroads of trade routes leading to the Middle East, Central Asia and India. She also went to the blue mosque at Mazar-e-Sharif and to Hadda, a Greco-Buddhist site located in Gandhara near the Khyber Pass. One of her fondest memories is of travelling to Jalalabad to meet Khan Abdul Ghaffar Khan.

Excitement, joy, more excitement, this is what I felt. I had grown up on stories of his extraordinary unarmed army of Red Shirts.[2] Meeting him in the garden of his house in Sheesham Bagh was wonderful. He was over 'eighty, tall and gaunt with a crinkly-eyed smile on his long famous face, followed by a certain reticent sadness when he spoke about his long detention in Pakistan. He reminded me of my grandfather. Staunch Gandhians, they were similar in indefinable ways.

Another trip that left an indelible imprint was to the archaeological remains of the Bamyan Valley, her second in quick succession. She spent time at the monastic ensembles and sanctuaries admiring the syncretic interplay of Indian, Hellenistic, Roman, Sasanian and Islamic influences, while the official team surveyed the restoration work being carried out by the Archaeological Survey of India. It was a wind-scoured trip—their entourage took the northern route and reached Bamyan carousing through the hairpin turns of the Shibar Pass, situated at a woozy 3,000 metres above sea level.

The return route was through barren, unpaved roads that seemed endless, till, wind-battered and bone-deep cold, the group reached Band-e-Amir, a confluence of six exquisite emerald-blue lakes. Enthralled by the beauty of the lakes, under a romantic, star-sprinkled night sky, Sonal surprised and enchanted her little group by performing an impromptu dance inspired by the karanas portrayed in the Tanjore and Chidambaram temples. There were no accoutrements but the magical experience was an unmissable one for everyone present there.

> I had so much fun that night. I danced for a long, long time and everyone watched with absolute delight.

Memories, dreams, desires, needs—Sonal was dealing with all this and more. Her efforts to make her marriage work were faltering. Her personal spaces were getting increasingly recriminatory. There were many emotionally charged moments, trivial in isolation but accreting into something she found difficult to deal with. She crawled into her own little circle of personal relationships and associations. There were picnics and barbecues with close friends. Salman Haider and his theatre-actress wife, Kusum, Paul Mathiew and his wife, Leela, the director of the Kabul Museum and his Japanese wife . . . Inflecting his reminiscences with nostalgia, Salman Haider recalls, 'We were close friends. It was a small mission with not a great deal of social life outside the mission. We spent a lot of time together. Sonal was a lively, dazzling presence. Her infectious gaiety drew even my two little children to her.'

> I learnt to make *polao* and *qorma*, a dish of stuffed onions called *osh pyozee* and *lavash* from the young Hazara couple working at my house, teaming this up with *bolani* (a flat

bread stuffed with either pumpkin, potato or green onions) bought from vendors sitting atop donkey carts heaving with melons and flattened bread. I learnt a smattering of Dari and spent many afternoons browsing through rare books at the museum library.

From Lalit, I craved nothing more than a cuddle! For me, shared laughter is indicative of a shared life, but we were not laughing together any more.

Not worrying about whether it would go down well with Lalit, once, after a long spell of inflammatory arguments, Sonal drove a Volkswagen borrowed from Paul's agency all the way up to the perilous Salang Pass, nestled at 11,000 feet in the Hindu Kush mountains. It was an extremely bumpy, rough ride between vast stretches of naked hills with high-velocity winds pushing insistently at her car. She stopped briefly whenever she felt tired, trying to create some culinary happiness for herself with local bread and fresh mint picked from nearby farms, eating slices of waxed pineapple, swapping jokes and anecdotes with fellow travellers.

I told them about my 1969 trip as part of Indira Gandhi's cultural delegation when, in the middle of a valley in the Hindu Kush, I broke my chappal. I was hungry, but being a diehard vegetarian, all I could get to eat were *aloo bukhara*s (plums)!

Sonal continued to perform in India during this period, downsizing her soaring celebrity status every time she returned to Kabul. In real time, this translated into several recitals in Delhi, a recital in Bombay at the Sabha Hall of the Shanmukhananda Fine Arts and Sangeet Sabha, another at the Kala Mandir in Calcutta, at Rabindra Bharati in Hyderabad, at the Jaipur festival, in several German cities, in Ankara, and at the Kalakshetra in Madras. And when asked by a journalist about her husband's response to her increasing dance commitments, she laughingly replied, 'One can get a good wife. Is it not difficult to get a good dancer in a wife?'

Sonal's performance at Kalakshetra, the Mecca of classical Indian dance, caught the attention of Rukmini Devi. In a treasured letter written to Sonal on 7 January 1971, Rukmini wrote,

> This is just to tell you that I was very happy that you came and gave the performance here that was a great success. Everyone enjoyed your recital very much. I would also like to tell you that I appreciated your recital and I can see how hard you have worked to get your technique perfect. Your expressions even in Sringara Rasa were so dignified and without any vulgarity it had a special appeal to me.

Sonal was in blazing form. Her beauty dazzled. Her performances seized the audience. Her recital at Shanmukhananda Sabha was acclaimed for its intellectual approach, and the newness and freshness that Sonal seemed to have brought to the traditional Bharatanatyam and Odissi repertory. She seemed to have almost an instinctive feel for the ebb and flow of each dance movement. Her expressive face teased out details of abhinaya beautifully. She also had the lovely knack of explaining her movements, of narrating the story. Dance critics found her rendering of an elaborate varnam in *Sankarabharanam*[3] exquisite. Equally exquisite was her rendering of the Gati Bheda Pallavi and two ashtapadis of Jayadeva, 'Pashyati Dishi Dishi' and 'Kuru Yadunandana', with the 'Moksha Nritya' or the dance of liberation forming a gripping finale to the Odissi part of her recital.

Sonal's maiden performance at Calcutta at Kala Mandir too was an evening of three hours of rapturous delight and frequent standing ovations. According to the dance critic of *Hindustan Standard*,

> The Varnam in Raga Nattiakurinji was the highlight of the day. The piece was embellished by Sonal's gazelle-like grace over a wide range of speed and she portrayed the theme most effectively so as to permeate the hearts of the audience. Her impeccable sense of rhythm was once again revealed in the fast paced Tillana, which seemed to trigger the whole atmosphere and had the audience spellbound.[4]

She danced superb Bharatanatyam and Odissi solos at the Convention Hall of the Ashoka in Delhi. After one such performance, the art critic of *The Statesman* wrote,

> Her Varnam recorded a dramatic eye-witness account of Gajendra Moksham[5] from a ring-side seat, as well as a poignant narration of Draupadi's discomfiture which turned into Dussasana's doom as he tried to disrobe her in the Kaurava court.[6] Both these episodes were rendered with excellent abhinaya and breathtaking footwork.

She followed with a tillana that she herself choreographed, climaxed by an exciting rhythmic competition between her feet and the mridangam and ghatam.[7] The recital ended in a clever manipulation of the time-cycles, and Sonal froze into the sculptured images of South Indian temples with marvellous effect.[8] The Odissi part of the recital that included an original composition from Ramcharitmanas, compiled by Dr Suresh Awasthi, called 'Phulwari Leela' was also a tour de force.

The year 1971 was one of political and cultural activism. George Harrison and Ravi Shankar teamed up to organize the Concert for Bangladesh in New York's Madison Square to focus on the heart-rending refugee issue. Devastated by the extent of genocide in Bangladesh, Sonal participated in sit-ins and tried to collect money for refugees who had crossed over to India.

I stood for hours holding a placard on a footpath in Connaught Place and then went into several restaurants full of smoke and noise to motivate people to donate.

She also performed to help raise funds for the National Defence Fund, teaming up with Indrani Rahman and Birju Maharaj for a performance at the Ashoka as well as the Hindon airbase and the air force station at Agra.

Sonal was clearly the girl of the moment, celebrated in photo shoots and press reports, the darling of the most sceptical of art critics and cultural czars, fuelling a cultural paparazzi rush unrivalled in its time. Not so at home in Kabul, where dark truths lurked. The city she had grown to love had turned into one of smoke and mirrors presenting a passel of surprises, one of them being that all the contradictions and ambiguities in her marriage that she had desperately tried to work on were off the boil. There were unpleasant altercations that she could not deal with.

It was clear by now that our relationship had run its course. I tried, but couldn't make it work. Lalit needed a wife who would support his social and diplomatic commitments. He was very keen to start a family and needed a mother for his children. And then, one summer night in 1972, a violent argument following a dinner engagement at the Indian ambassador's residence was the proverbial final straw.

In the afternoon that same day, the ambassador's wife, Sakeena, had asked me to come over to her place to make samosas and sandwiches. I was in a meeting with the museum director. I told her that it was not possible for me to leave the meeting. She was absolutely livid. Later that evening, Sakeena told Lalit that I was rocking his foreign service boat. Lalit more than endorsed this view, more so when we were by ourselves at home. 'My ambassador's wife thinks you are not good for my career,' he said.

That night had all the clamminess of a bad dream. I kept expecting Lalit to apologize for his feckless behaviour, his acts of contrition, but he made absolutely no overture. Deeply hurt, I packed and drove to the airport in a taxi that Salman managed to fix for me the next morning.

* * *

We are listening to an amateur band playing chunks of Mozart's String Quartet.

Was it anything like Bergman's *Scenes from a Marriage*?[9]

I certainly did not pattern it on that. I think Bergman's scenes of disintegration of a marriage came a year later, in 1973, and resulted in spikes in divorce rates, especially in Scandinavia. I certainly was not like Marianne in any way, not even like a protagonist from a Russian novel, seesawing between ecstasy and despair. I never reached out to tranquillizers and barbiturates.

In many ways an outsider, I feel that my sense of belonging within this marriage was, after a point, counterbalanced by an equal sense of non-belonging.

Did this help you cope better? Were there any 'mad woman in the attic' moments?

I don't know about the mad woman, but certainly an angry one, an extremely sad one *(laughs)*.

The fact that you've retained his name piqued the media's interest and turned your divorce into a subject of scrutiny.

What's in a name? *(laughs again)* The name has worked well, hasn't it? It has been a good fit.

You have been fairly tight-lipped about your personal life. Was it a bitter uncoupling? What led to the final parting? Infidelity? Unrequited love?

No, it happened because I refused to live a formulaic life as a junior diplomat's wife. I was giving hundreds of performances, rehearsing for hours, travelling. I was extremely focused on dance. My passion for dance was seen as some sort of an unforgivable quirk, a grave flaw, evidence of my egocentricity, my immutability, even a form of subversion.

What did you do to provoke the ambassador's wife's fury?

I challenged the status quo. Her reaction was perhaps typical of that time and milieu. As a junior diplomat's wife, I was expected to be mindlessly compliant.

You also had to sidestep accusations of vanity.

I was being bludgeoned for my commitment to dance.

Was it vain to want to dance? Lalit found me in dance. There was never any undertaking to give up or curtail dancing!

7

New Beginnings

The news that Lalit and Sonal were headed for divorce gained traction when Sonal returned to India. It brought in a degree of notoriety, played out in the gaze of the media. Clichéd, distorted versions of what might have gone wrong were going viral. There were stories of secret liaisons, of bizarre misunderstandings. Heads would turn and conversations would awkwardly stop when she entered a room. It was a dark, unsettling phase, harrowing too, because of unbelievable attacks from unexpected quarters.

Sonal's parents were shocked at the news and felt she had not done enough to stave off the split. Even though her mother's initial foreboding about her relationship with Lalit was prescient, the finality of their separation was too much for her to handle. 'You are not my daughter!' she raged. 'I shall have nothing to do with you any more.' Caustic and unforgiving, she kept to her word for six long years. Sonal's father too clammed up. For him, Lalit would remain the ideal *jamai babu.*[1]

Sonal's relationships in tatters, there were a multitude of 'hurts' to deal with. The cruellest whiplash, and one that perhaps bruised her the most, came from her guru, Kelucharan Mohapatra.

I reached out to him as soon as I got back. A guru is like a father. I expected him to empathize with me, to help me deal with the trauma of separation, but he behaved with monstrous egotism. He not only mocked me, but kicked my head when I bent down to touch his feet.

Coping with the shadow caused by her guru's rejection was not easy. She was ostracized by reigning cultural cliques and had to deal with tabloid columns peppered with lacerating barbs. Sleepless nights turgid with anxiety followed.

* * *

We are sitting at a sun-dappled table in a little garden restaurant, reminiscing about those difficult days.

How did you cope with the downpour of so much vitriol?

What I faced was humiliating, banal, low. I can still feel that catch in the throat, that tightness of lungs, when I pleaded with my guru to restore our relationship, but it was pointless. Even his silence had a corrosive quality. And then I had to deal with the pile-up of clichés. People were treating my separation from Lalit as carte blanche to mock me, to question my values, even to question the authenticity of my dance.

In a sense, that period spelt the end of the first act of my life. What troubled me also was the impact of our separation on my father-in-law. He loved me deeply. I am sure, at some level, my decision to leave Lalit broke his heart. The news of his death in Cuttack a year later completely shook me.

You must have been in an all-time low simmer of moods.

For some time it was difficult to look beyond the feeling of pain and loss, of abandonment and rejection. It needed some amount of courage to begin again. This was when I turned to my mentor, Jiwan Pani. He had moved to Delhi for a stint at the Sangeet Natak Akademi. Strikingly perceptive about what I was going through, he gave me the non-judgemental support I badly needed. It was like seeing a therapist. And then slowly, with his help, I packed away my emotional freight, resumed my practice sessions and got my endorphins pumping again. My apparent equanimity must have surprised my detractors.

* * *

Their creative partnership once again stirred the poetic imagination that gave wings to Sonal's Odissi repertory. She cannot remember when this partnership foundered even for a moment. Her conceptual grasp of Odissi aesthetics began to outstrip that of other prominent dancers. The distinctive musicality of her dance was enriched by Bankim Sethi, another close associate and vocal accompanist, the third point of the creative triangle. 'There were just a few ragas being used in compositions. We changed that and began using traditional ragas that had been somehow airbrushed from the Odissi dance consciousness. We began by studying more than half a dozen treatises written between the sixteenth and eighteenth centuries, and found that two of them—*Geet-Prakash* and *Sangeeta Narayana*[2]—clearly defined ragas distinct from the Carnatic and the Hindustani School,' recalls Bankim. 'We created some of the most spectacular dance music using traditional ragas like Deshakhya, Varadi, Malav and Prathama Manjari, Amra Pancham, Desh Varadi, Vasant and Shri.'

Sonal's Odissi repertory is formidable. In terms of numbers it translates into sixty-six mangalacharans, three *batus*—also called sthayis, seventeen pallavis, two mokshas, a *natangi*,[3] two dozen songs in Oriya and eighteen ashtapadis from the *Geet Govind*. What is significant is that Sonal has embraced the oral tradition of ashtapadis. In Jiwan Pani's words,

There are a few ashtapadis which are sung in Orissa very artistically, but the tunes do not conform to the indicated raga. Sonal has retained those tunes of the oral tradition. For instance, the 7th and the 19th ashtapadis are rendered in the same tune as are sung in the oral tradition. . . . Sonal spared no pains to delve deeper into the Vaishnava philosophy. She has also learnt Sanskrit. Therefore, her abhinaya of the ashtapadis makes for a rare aesthetic experience.[4]

New compositions continue to pour out of her. The choreographic chemistry at work has been equally astonishing. She has created twenty-one choreographies in Sanskrit, fifty-two in Hindi, thirty in Oriya and twenty-two in other languages. No one dares to call into question her depth of engagement with Odissi, an engagement that continues to surprise her audience time and again.

By 1973, Sonal was up for new challenges. Sensing her keenness to learn the Mayurbhanj style of Chhau,[5] Jiwan Pani managed to persuade one of Chhau's great gurus, Ananta Charan Sai, a Sangeet Natak Akademi awardee, to teach her. Guru Sai travelled from Baripada to Delhi with a *muhuri* or small shehnai player and a percussionist to play the dhol. For Sonal, this was the flowering of a dream. She had first seen a full-blown, visually arresting Mayurbhanj Chhau performance at the Chaitra Parva festival in Baripada in 1968. Dr Mayadhar Mansingh and Jiwan Pani were both at hand to explain the finer nuances of this part-folk, part-tribal, part-martial classical dance tradition.

> I remember being transfixed. I was learning and performing Odissi, which had a lyrical, predominantly lasya style. The overt masculine tandava element in Chhau complemented it beautifully. The tribhanga became *dharan*, one of the basic postures of Chhau. Chowka, the squatting posture, became more pronounced. The pirouettes, the basic steps, or *tapka*s, and the jumps, or *ufli*s, were spectacular.

The year went by in a blur of deadlines. Sonal learnt and practised with a teen-like zest, spending four hours in the morning and two in the late afternoon and using tapes that were worn out from playing over and over again, not resting till she had mastered the style. Later, at one of her regular performances in Ashoka Theatre, she dedicated the second half to Mayurbhanj Chhau. She remembers the astonished silence and the huge applause that followed. This recital earned her the distinction of being the first woman dancer of Chhau.

There were other monumental issues that coloured Sonal's life at this point and made it look almost soap-operatic. To begin with, the small, cramped Curzon Road apartment (D 707) where she had sought temporary refuge was turned into a brothel by the caretaker during one of her European tours. Horror-struck, she left the place and lived for a while at the India International Centre, moving to different temporary shelters before taking refuge at John Lall's house in Jorbagh. She had claimed no alimony, so she had to scrimp and save every paisa of her earnings from recitals to clear huge penal rent bills of the Curzon Road apartment[6] and to meet her personal expenses. She remembers taking overdrafts from her bank, selling off gold bangles gifted by her mother and borrowing money from well-wishers like O.P. Jain[7] and A.J. Jaspal[8] to pay her musicians.

Sonal continued to spend many homeless nights in the city with most of her possessions in Muhammad Yunus's[9] garage, taking shelter even in the nondescript little Lakshmibai Nagar flat of her Bharatanatyam vocalist, Kamakshi Kuppuswamy. Finally, her friends, Rajgopal and his wife Maithili, invited her to share their Shahjahan Road flat and she stayed there off and on for nearly three years. After her gilded earlier life, this was austere business.

The quiet struggle against daunting odds was carried out without a trace of bitterness, and what appeared as awful loose ends and ambiguities ended up becoming Sonal's strengths. No longer entombed in a dead relationship, she began revving up her personal life and expanding her circle of friends. She had a coterie of dazzled, starry-eyed admirers and dozens of playful relationships. She began building some meaningful relationships as well, spending a good deal of time with cultural icons like Kamaladevi Chattopadhyay.[10] This set the artistic and emotional tone of a new period of her life.

> Kamaladevi was my inspiration. I called her 'Amma'. Her home in Canning Lane, which I used to visit frequently, was an adda for writers, craftspersons and activists from the cooperative, socialist and feminist movements. The intellectual, artistic churning that went on at Amma's place helped me regain my innate cool and confidence.

Sonal was invited back to the stage. She performed with dizzying frequency and remained in the news for brilliant, hugely acclaimed, rousing performances that few of her contemporaries could equal. She looked gorgeous, and her down-to-earth, unstarry style quotient continued to draw the attention of fashion columnists. Her hair pulled back in a topknot or cascading down her back, her turtleneck sweaters, handwoven sarees, kumkum-dotted forehead, her full lips, dark berry or red with the reddest of lipsticks, and kohl-lined eyes set off a trend.

It was around this time that Georg Lechner, whom she teasingly called 'Snoopy', waltzed into Sonal's life. Georg was the director of Max Mueller Bhawan in New Delhi. One of Sonal's favourite anecdotes is about their first meeting.

Preparations for the 1972 Olympics in Munich were on in full swing.

I received a call from the Max Mueller Bhawan to do a photo session with a famous German photographer for the non-German cultural shows to be presented during the Olympiad. I remember reaching slightly late because Kelu Sir would not leave until my eyes and eyebrows were painted by him with just the right arch and every hair was in place. And there was Dr Lechner, arms folded on chest, looking like a lion about to roar. However, by the time the shoot ended, he made it abundantly clear that he couldn't wait to see me again.

Kumkum corroborates. 'Sonal was a ravishing beauty. We saw Georg's attraction turn into obsession.'

What followed was a season of uncontrollable longing. Georg was married with two children, but that did not stop them from beginning an affair that was the talk of the town. Neither of them tried to quell the swirling gossip. It was an open liaison that played out in public spaces. It was not long before then prime minister Indira Gandhi got a whiff of the brewing scandal and, according to Sonal, managed to use her influence to get Georg posted to the Goethe-Institut Montreal.

This was the summertime of Sonal's performances, a period when she travelled to different parts of Europe with or without Georg, but always with her Bharatanatyam and Odissi musicians, through vast stretches of green vineyards and forest-cloaked hills to cities with rich cultural histories and stunning architecture. Georg arranged for her to dance at interesting festivals such as the Europaische Wochen in Passau and the Bayreuth Youth Festival, the Mecca of German opera which draws Wagner enthusiasts from around the world.

Bayreuth stretched her in ways she had not anticipated.

I learnt to appreciate the beauty of the libretto, enjoy the verve of jazz. I feasted on Wagner's operas, sitting for hours on a wooden seat in the Festspielhaus, awestruck by *Der Ring des Nibelungen*, scores featuring *Der Fliegende Holländer*, the hugely moving *Tristan and Isolde* and Wagner's swan song, *Parsifal*—letting the music wash over me, not getting out of the opera house in much under five hours. I turned into a complete Wagnerphile.

The couple was caught in the sunshine of creative, happy days, stopping at tourist-thronged city centres to eat warm slices of apple strudel and buttered pretzels bought from roadside vendors. If they as much as stepped into a fancy restaurant and were lucky to secure a table, Sonal's vegetarianism would end up causing a great deal of mirth. Georg would try and explain in chaste German, 'Please, no fish, no meat, no pig, no game, only salad!' The friendly and attentive waiters would nod in comprehension and reappear with different kinds of greens.

My suspicious fork had however learnt to ferret out tiny bits of bacon and sausages hidden in salad leaves. When summoned to explain, the staff would smilingly exclaim, 'Oh, that tiny piece!' I would end up munching their delicious buttered loaves and strudels and mounds of ice cream.

In an alien land, no longer ambushed by rumours of improprieties, Sonal experienced the joy and feverish excitement that had eluded her for a long time. Georg and she were compatible, had similar interests. 'I must confess,' she said in a letter to Kumkum, 'I am so happy and fulfilled with Georg that sometimes I don't wish to think about the difficulties I face in Delhi.' In another letter written during the same time, she wrote, 'You must realize how much I miss India, my dance, the atmosphere, although I have gained something terribly important here, Georg's love and many valuable friendships.'

It was evident that Georg was doing his best to help her fall in love with Germans and Germany. Conversations revolved around German dance, music, poetry and philosophy, the similarity between the ideas of Kant, Hegel, Nietzsche, Schopenhauer and the Indian philosophers. Travelling through the heritage cities of Nuremberg, Wurzburg, Kulmbach and German villages nestling in lovely forests and hills, he took her to quaint little wine bars and country cellars for walk-in tastings of the best of their vintage wines. There was a playful eclecticism in Georg's choice of theatre performances, of movies, of concerts. Sonal was hooked.

Lalit and Sonal filed for divorce by mutual consent in 1973. In a sense, the final breakup wasn't tumultuous or contentious. Sonal did not seek spousal support. In 1974, when the Tis Hazari Court[11] granted them divorce, she decided to ring in her new life in style.

Lalit and I took a taxi and went to Connaught Place. I first went into a saree shop and bought myself a bright pink silk saree with a quaint purple-blue design and an orange border. After that I took Lalit to the Standard Restaurant for lunch. The restaurant was packed but we managed to secure a table and were for some time our old, happy selves. The fact that we weren't going to be at loggerheads any more needed to be celebrated.

Georg too got his divorce the same year.

8

Born Again

Life is not about waiting for the storm to pass
It's about learning to dance in the rain.

—Vivian Greene

On 24 August 1974, Sonal had a close brush with death. She was being driven back from Nuremberg to Bayreuth by Georg after spending a 'delightful day' with their artist friend, Herbert Traue. It was a wet, lacquer-dark night on a deserted autobahn near the town of Pegnitz where there was no speed limit and one could drive as fast as one liked. In love, and heady like a teenager, Sonal was humming a peppy song, when the car's headlight unexpectedly picked on a deer standing in the middle of the road. Georg slammed the brakes hard, but their Volkswagen Beetle skidded on the rain-drenched road, did three somersaults, turned upside down and settled on its roof. Sonal lost consciousness as she was tossed 4 metres away from the car on the hard surface of the motorway.

Sonal threads together the events of that terrible night and all that followed.

My flight through air and the impact of the fall rendered me unconscious. Georg escaped with only a whiplash injury on the neck. Luckily, a passing car called the police from a roadside phone. A sprinkle of water and I came to, murmuring, 'I am cold.' My blue Pashmina shawl covered me as I was gently lifted by a male nurse into an ambulance from the nearby town of Pegnitz.

After preliminary investigations at the Pegnitz General Hospital, she was referred to the University Clinic of Erlangen, near Nuremberg, a city known for its specialized clinics and hospitals.

X-rays revealed that four of her ribs were badly damaged, her twelfth vertebra was smashed to smithereens and both her collarbones were broken. Was it the final act, a denouement that even her worst nightmares had not prepared her for? Trapped within a carapace of pain, her limp body lay under the hot lights of the OT where the treating orthopaedic surgeons gave her two options—to allow them to insert a steel rod in her back to hold up the spine, or to shroud the body with a heavy plaster cast to allow nature to heal her body. Impetuously, she chose the latter option.

During the two weeks at this clinic, support came from unexpected quarters. An Indian woman, Vrinda Swatek, married to a Czech German, visited her every day with food with Indian flavours.

Dressed in a lovely silk sari with a big round bindi and salt-and-pepper hair, her presence was so comforting. She

Sonal in her grandfather's lap

Sonal as Cupid (Raj Bhawan, Nagpur, 1950)

Dancing Manipuri

With sister, Arti: The lotus and the bee

Music group (from left): Sonal; mother, Poornima; sister, Arti

Family portrait (from left): sister, Arti; brother, Anuj; father, Arvind; grandfather, Mangaldas Pakvasa; mother, Poornima; and Sonal (Raj Bhawan, Nagpur, 1952)

Gujarati folk dance (Elphinstone College, Bombay)

Sonal's arangetram (Raj Bhawan, Bangalore, 1961)

With musicians and her Bharatanatyam gurus, Professor U.S. Krishna Rao (fourth from left) and Chandrabhaga Devi (fifth from right), at her arangetram

Bharatanatyam performance (Madras, 1962)

The lotus and the bee mudra, Bharatanatyam

During a Bharatanatyam lec-dem in Zurich

With her Odissi guru Kelucharan Mohapatra (extreme right) (Cuttack, 1968)

Odissi performance at the Museum Theatre in Madras in the late 1960s (left to right): Kelucharan Mohapatra, Rukmini Devi, Sonal, M.S. Subbulakshmi, Sadasivam and Y.G. Doraiswamy

Among temple ruins at the Qutb Minar, Delhi

Beckoning her lover, Bharatanatyam

Odissi portrait

Konark nayika, Odissi

Demonstration of the
tribhanga at an Odissi workshop

Swan, Bharatanatyam

In the early days of b/w television
in India

Performance at the Expo '70 (Osaka)

Odissi abhinaya

Holding the veena, Odissi

Parshva mardala, Odissi

Odissi at the Tughlaqabad Fort, Delhi

Classical beauty

Throwing down the gauntlet

Post-recovery Bharatanatyam performance at the Convention
Hall at Hotel Ashoka (Delhi, 1975)

An Odissi lec-dem

Performing Bharatanatyam at the
Bayreuth Festival in Germany

Maria Magdalena (Mexico, 1979)

Kiss, Odissi

Krishna, Odissi

Striking a pose at the Chanakyapuri
residence of friend Peter Curtis, the
Australian high commissioner to India

Kalki, Odissi (Konark)

Ram, Bharatanatyam

With friend Arjun Puri (Auroville)

Receiving the Padma Bhushan from former President, R. Venkataraman (Delhi, 1992)

With her disciples at the Centre for Indian Classical Dances (CICD, Delhi)

Teaching at the CICD

With mentor Jiwan Pani

Geometry in Bharatanatyam

Setting the stage on fire as Draupadi (1994)

Stunning as Draupadi

Workshop at the Tihar Jail (Delhi, 1998)

Kargil, 1999

With close friend Veena Shroff

Performing on the International Dance Day (Paris, 2001)

Giving a lecture at McGill University (Montreal, 2001)

With friend Suchi (extreme left) and others in London

With Pandit Ravi Shankar

An Odissi moment

Asmita, contemporary choreography (Delhi, 2002)

A still from Prakash Jha's film, *Sonal* (2002)

Receiving the Padma Vibhushan from former President,
Dr A.P.J. Abdul Kalam (Delhi, 2003)

A still from the Doordarshan dance reality show *Rum Jhum*, 2013

Indo-Greek production, *When the Gods Meet* (2013)

Solo dance-theatre, *Stree,* presented on International
Women's Day (Delhi, 8 March 2016)

would bring along a silver thali, katoris, spoon, napkin, glass and delicious food! She fed me roti, dal, sabzi, salad, dahi.[1]

Dr Vollmar, the treating physician at Hof, gave Sonal exceptional personal attention. Georg was by her side from morning till night.

It was not the pain, overwhelming as it was, that seared her. She overheard one of the doctors tell Georg that it would take several months of physiotherapy before she could walk. Returning to dance seemed improbable. For Sonal, this was like having her pause buttons permanently pushed.

My mind was in a whirl of unknown fears, doubts and ominous signals. Images of my own dances on prestigious stages of national theatres and opera houses kept flashing before my eyes. Was all this just a bad dream?

It was a frozen time for her, and newspapers, magazines and radios the world over carried obituaries to her career in dance. Letters, messages and telegrams poured in from known and unknown people and places. Indira Gandhi's was one of the first, asking her to keep her chin up. 'India prays for you,' read the message in her telegram.

Fourteen days after the accident, Sonal was moved to Montreal where Georg worked. Her Air Canada flight was also shot through with some amount of drama. She was to board the flight at the Frankfurt airport.

As my ambulance came to a halt just in front of the nose of the plane, the pilots saw the vehicle. The doors opened and the captain stood there, arms firmly crossed at the chest as I slid down on the stretcher. I still remember every detail of that moment when he looked down at me strapped to the stretcher and told Lechner, 'We can't take her. We are not prepared for this.' I was looking up at him as a sacrificial goat might at its rescuer. Even that did not help. Lechner whispered to the two male nurses to unstrap me and haul me up. I staggered up the forty-odd steps of the ladder helped by those two and greeted the captain with a dazzling smile and a 'Good afternoon, Captain, thank you!' I still don't know how I did it. It was almost like climbing Mount Everest without oxygen.

With no readymade protocol or blueprint for dealing with her condition, Sonal put all her grit together to survive the fourteen-hour transatlantic flight ordeal, with just a small halt at the Shannon airport in Ireland. She sat in her narrow economy seat obsessing about keeping her posture right, with only two tiny cushions for support, her antennae sensitive to the curious glances of the other passengers when she walked mannequin-like to the washroom assisted by Georg.

I was dressed in a billowing, unbecoming tank top and skirt, my torso square and rigid with the neck to hip plaster cast weighing four kilos, supported by a blond man with green eyes. There were speculations on whether I belonged to Greece, Italy or Mexico.

Sonal remembers that flight most also for the intimate camaraderie between her and Georg and the captain's thoughtfulness in ensuring that she was served bread, cheese and desserts from the first-class menu.

Georg's apartment in Montreal was on the ninth floor of a building called the Port-Royal on 1455, Sherbrooke, a road lined with bars, boutiques, antique-stores and art galleries. Sonal, confined to bed and dealing with dark interior monologues and haunted by reminiscences, was getting to a point where she wanted to dismantle her memories, the pointless reveries of the past. To think that all this was happening to her, a woman who exulted in her body, and more than that, in her dance.

And there was poor Georg trying to nurse me, sublimating his restless intensity, assisted by a German-teaching couple from the Goethe-Institut, Bernhard and Hildegard Beutler, who took turns to look after me. Lying on my back in the quiet isolation of my room, trying to block out sounds from the legendary Ritz Carlton that was just across the road and where Elizabeth Taylor and Richard Burton had once got married, I felt as brittle as a glass doll.

I could move only my fingers and eyes. I went through all the hasta mudras a number of times, did eye exercises like a Kathakali dancer and recreated the accident and the ensuing events with just those gestures and eye movements. Nothing assuaged my feeling of impending doom. Whispers from the living room from where phone calls were made and received reconfirmed what the German doctors had said, 'She will never dance again!'[2]

It was in Montreal that a well-known chiropractor, Dr Pierre Gravel, who had seen her give a lec-dem a couple of months ago at the Goethe-Institut, took up the challenge of bringing her back to her feet. He was vacationing in the beautiful Laurentian Mountains, about three hours' drive from Montreal, when he received news about the accident and drove straight back to see her.

He confessed that he usually would not disturb his well-earned summer holiday for anything, but when he was told that it was the Indian dancer he had seen a few months ago and she had broken her back in a terrible accident, he dropped his yacht on the lake, his girlfriend, Myrto, and cats in the chalet, and drove down to see me. He told me how he was himself a music buff and how profoundly he was moved by Indian dance that evening when he had seen me perform.

Pierre turned her room into an intensive care cubicle, beginning his diagnostics with a bunch of x-rays. A couple of days into his investigations and after holding consultations with leading orthopaedics and surgeons on the exact damage to the vertebrae, he stood at the foot of her bed looking rather grim. 'I am afraid,' he said with a dramatic pause, and as if fearing the worst, she looked into his warm, compassionate, deeply intimate, blue eyes, her own welling with tears, 'I am afraid that you will be able to dance again.' Even though she was crying, nothing could dilute the adrenalin that Pierre's simple words generated. The days spent in despair paled to monochrome in an instant, ready to be filed in neatly in her catalogue of memories, and pushed away.

Sensing what I was going through, Pierre caressed my hair and held my hand, which he was to hold all through the arduous journey back to a life of dancing. 'But it will be hard work, Sonal,' he said. 'You will have to promise to follow everything I say.' I was ready to stand on my head if he delivered on his promise.

More importantly, Sonal promised herself that no matter what it would take, she would reclaim her life. This was the beginning of the process of what she loves to call her 'second birth'.

In a letter addressed to Kumkum on 18 September, Sonal wrote with her characteristic cast-iron self-assurance. 'Contrary to very annoying newspaper and radio reports, the doctors assure me that I can go back to the stage after six months, but make no secret of the patience and discipline it will require. I hope I have both in adequate measure and praise my destiny that the accident has treated me the way it has, since I hear that even a slightly different angle during my fall could have paralysed me.'

Sonal could not bend or lift even her toe without wolf-howls but had to follow a rigid protocol set by Pierre. Slowly she graduated to being propped up in bed. Anuj, her brother, dispatched from Bombay by her parents, was her chief nurse during this time.

He stayed for four months nursing me, driving Georg to his office, getting groceries, learning to use the washing machine and doing a bit of cooking. His sense of humour helped me laugh and filled my broken ribs with happy oxygen. He was there through the bitter Montreal winter when on certain days the temperature would drop to –35°C at night. He learnt to enjoy wine and cheese, make masala omelettes and generally feel at home in fashionable Montreal.

Sunshine was back in Sonal's life. She was learning to take a few steps, was assisted to the large glass windows of her living room to gaze at the Montreal skyline and to look at the dancing lights in the street below. She read the entire works of Anais Nin, reread the account of Han Suyin's affair in Hong Kong with the journalist Ian Morrison in *A Many-Splendoured Thing*, reread also Thomas Mann's *Buddenbrooks*. She wrote letters to her friends and rejoiced in their love and prayers.

Throughout winter, I was clad in the plaster cast and loose shorts. One long loose cardigan and a warm overcoat, muffler and knee-length socks would augment my costume for visits to Pierre's clinic. I could still not lift arms to do my hair, so whoever was at hand—the weekly cleaning lady, a visitor or Lechner—would try to comb my long hair. Most of the time I looked like a strange creature out of Humpty Dumpty or Grimm's fairy tales.

Pierre was not one to let me off the hook. He prescribed toe–ankle–knee wiggling exercises. He asked me to stand in front of the mirror to practise my facial expressions; eyes, eyebrows, nostrils, mouth, neck. His clinic had also become my workshop, where, as I sipped sherry, he and the staff buzzed in and out of my corner room to learn moving the eyebrows, bend fingers in a simple mudra, and glide their neck sideways. It provided me with so much fun and mirth just to see them make funny faces and move their derrière instead of neck. Their eyes went in every direction, and eyebrows refused to budge from their God-given placement. So, the months passed and as I picked up strength in my legs, arms and mind, I began dreaming. The hours were more profitably spent in mentally going through my repertory of Bharatanatyam and Odissi.

The heavy cast imprisoning her body was removed on a cold weekend in November. Pierre invited her to listen to some rare recordings at his clinic from his amazing collection of Western classical music, but when she arrived, he took a quick x-ray and asked her to stretch out on the traction table in a corner of the room. While Georg engaged her in some trivia, Pierre used a soundless electric saw to rip off her cast.

I lay there half-naked, two big pieces of the cast hanging loose on two sides. For a long moment I stared in space. No one spoke. Then I let out a high-pitched wail, sobbing my heart out.

Pierre coaxed her to drink some cognac to calm her down. She was then treated to a luxurious bubble bath. She wallowed in their tender affection as both Georg and Pierre set to wash her with aromatic gels, shampooing and combing out her coxcomb of tangled hair.

That moment of iridescent joy was celebrated with a bottle of vintage Dom Pérignon champagne, canapés from a bakery, and a large salmon brought in especially from the Gaspésie Lake renowned for its amazing salmon. Eating the salmon was Sonal's initiation into non-vegetarianism.

Having been brought up as a strict vegetarian, I squirmed at the thought of eating flesh. Yet how could I ignore my doctor's advice? My body had lost most of its protein base and a vegetarian diet was thoroughly ill-equipped to restore that loss. I prepared myself mentally to bite into the salmon and almost passed out at the offensive smell. The doctor started to count. Finally, I pushed that yucky thing down my throat and literally washed it down with ten goblets of champagne. The afternoon ended with the screening of Walt Disney films, *Ferdinand the Bull*, *Three Little Pigs* and *Tom and Jerry*—taking them all back to the raucous laughter and the joy and naiveté of when they were children. Later that evening, Pierre and Myrto took Sonal and Georg to the best Italian restaurant in town where she feasted, smoked her favourite Cuban cigar, Cohiba, and felt that the world was her oyster.

Recovery came with a set of unique challenges.

After a week of feasting and enjoying my castless body, on an evening visit to us, Pierre asked me to stand up and take a dance step. He asked me to remember that first day when I had been introduced to my first dance teacher and the first thing I learnt. With cocky self-confidence, I got up and took position in front of an expectant audience. I took the half-seated *ardha-mandali* position with hands on waist, feeling already like my old self. Then I tried to lift my right foot to strike the first mnemonic syllable, *taiya*. I fell down. I sat on the floor in utter shock. Pierre gently lifted me up. My eyes filled up. I was speechless.

Even though I was rid of the heavy cast, the burden of the truth that I could not even lift my foot, leave alone take a dance step, was heavier than anything I have ever felt. My cockiness vanished forever.

Months of gruelling physiotherapy followed under Pierre's supervision. It was a Herculean task to get her muscles, which were in a state of stasis, to move. Pierre began with three-minute slots, increased them to five minutes and then one hour, thrice a day. Extreme pain used to tear through her body every time she tried to lift a limb. But she persevered, and six months into the accident, began to take baby steps. Even getting her legs to bend for the *armandi*[3] seemed really difficult initially, but as Paulo Coelho said in *The Alchemist*, 'And, when you want something, all the universe conspires in helping you to achieve it.' And that's what happened eventually.

After many faltering wobbles, her torso, hips and legs remembered what they had to do. She began training seriously to the pounding beats of taped music, sometimes not even breaking for tea or lunch, getting her teeth into 'full items' with a sense of absolute madness and grit, bringing out recordings of her programmes in old-fashioned tapes winding on a spool on a Grundig recorder. A letter written to Kumkum on 22 February 1975 says it all: 'I am dancing again! Bless my stars and bless my doctor. He is an absolute angel. It seems I have made case history and my x-rays are sent now to universities and clinics for study! I do vigorous exercises, yoga, and have begun to dance from last week. You ask me about my routine—well, lots of work on myself, receptions, dinners (at home and out), friends, music and books.'

Through it all, Pierre was her tender, supportive partner. It was not much later that the Dawson College, just west of downtown Montreal, invited her to perform. Sonal was ecstatic. Her half-hour performance won her a standing ovation. At home, a huge basket of beautiful flowers and a box of chocolates awaited her. It was from Pierre and Myrto with a note that said, 'Hurray! You did it!' Sonal's presence henceforth was marked in Montreal's social and cultural life, and she was followed by the cultural paparazzi wherever she went.

9

The Arc Lights

Sonal returned to India in March 1975. She flew into Bombay to spend a week with her parents but stayed a little longer, interspersing her stay with a recital at Rang Bhawan, an open theatre at Dhobi Talao in south Bombay. The recital planned on 20 April, eight months after her accident, was preceded by an extraordinary amount of vitriol from a section of the cultural glitterati who doubted her ability to dance again. Ignoring the negativity around her, her silence as powerful a retort as any, Sonal quietly prepared for her post-accident Indian debut.

When she began her performance, there was a hushed, almost reverential silence, since everyone present knew about her accident. As beautiful as ever, she gave an exquisitely calibrated performance that had both the critics and the audience rooting for more.

It was so emotional. Everyone wanted to walk onstage to touch me, to hug me. This included Sitara Devi, the legendary Kathak maestro, who is also one of my inspirations. She ripped off a black thread coiled around her neck and tied it to mine to ward off the evil eye. It was an intimate, precious moment. We both had tears in our eyes.[1]

The Rang Bhawan performance was followed by a recital in Delhi at the Convention Hall at Hotel Ashoka on 4 May. Sonal was performing in Delhi for the first time after her much-publicized accident. Her loyal entourage of musicians was present at the airport to receive her. It was a feted performance in front of connoisseurs of the performing arts, diplomats, celebrities. Sonal danced the full Bharatanatyam margam for nearly two-and-a-half hours. Her repertory included one of the most demanding varnams in Bharatanatyam, the Navaragamalika Varnam,[2] a gem of the Pandanallur repertory. Visually stunning, her performance was once again a deeply emotive experience. When she bowed out, the unabated appreciation that followed not only set to rest all the catty chatter about her full recovery but also re-established her as one of the leading performers of the time.

Some in the audience saw arcs of light as I danced. Some said they didn't see me, only the dance . . . Unconscious of all this, I danced to my heart's content. I was back where I belonged.

It was clear that no one could at this point match Sonal's starry eminence. An avalanche of invitations followed from groups and institutions in India and abroad. Connecting dances that were seen as genre oddballs, Sonal danced to Bharatanatyam, Odissi and Chhau compositions, creating magic wherever she went. She danced at the Magha Mela in Allahabad, the Krishna festival at Vrindavan, the Dussehra festival at Kullu, the Shivaratri festival at Mandi, Sangeet Natak Akademi festivals all over India, the Brihadeeswara festival at Thanjavur and the Ramayana festival at Chitrakoot, to name but just a few. She also danced in festivals in Iran, Thailand, Brazil, the USSR, Poland, Germany, the USA, the UK, France, Brazil, Venezuela, Panama, Mexico and Nicaragua.

She performed in Iran in successive years beginning in 1974, when she went to Tehran as part of a cultural delegation led by then prime minister Indira Gandhi. She remembers being followed by star-struck admirers even when she picnicked with friends in the Honarmandan artists' park, eating a clay pot of white bean and potato stew while others dug into the local *aab-gosht* mutton curry. Her performance at a festival in Shiraz, the exquisite city of Saadi and Hafiz, has been documented lovingly by her close friend, Jasleen Dhamija. The year was 1977. Jasleen, then positioned as the ILO chief in Tehran, accompanied Sonal to her open-air recital at the Bagh-e-Aram. 'We watched her create a unity with the elements, we were one with her, with the rhythm of the music, with the floating melody of the flute, with the silent, ancient cypresses and with the moon in the sky. There was pin-drop silence, and everyone absorbed this experience and has treasured it ever since.'

In the early weeks of July 1975, Sonal and Georg flew back to Montreal for a post-recovery follow-up with Dr Pierre Gravel.

As promised, I reported back to Pierre who took a bunch of new x-rays and invited Georg and me to view them. He lit them up, hopped around, did a jig, hugged and kissed me and shed a tear as he pointed to the place where the twelfth vertebrae had been smashed to powder. I could not see any empty place because, as Pierre so excitedly said, a new bone like a bridge had grown connecting the eleventh and the thirteenth vertebrae! 'You demanded and nature provided,' he said. I gawked. Georg was confused. There on the x-ray panel was my own spine! Strong and supple, ready to undertake long journeys, sleepless nights on flights, trains or long roads, arduous solo recitals and much more.

On the personal front, the navarasa played out on stage became part of her life's minutiae of passion and calmness, joy and despair, anger and love. Her gypsy-like existence continued. She lived in borrowed space at Rajgopal and Maithili's Shahjahan Road flat, burrowed at the India International Centre periodically, hung out at John and Asha Lall's Jorbagh bungalow for months. As a result of her nomadic existence, several important letters and invitations to dance either got lost or reached her months later. Through all this, Georg was her arm candy. She married him on 3 August 1975 on a quiet morning at a registry in Montreal, wearing the same Oriya red-and-gold ikat saree that she had worn for her civil wedding with Lalit Mansingh.

Exuberant, Sonal spent a three-week period at Bayreuth performing and teaching dance to a group of forty young students from nine countries that included a few professional classical Western dancers. What she taught went beyond dance and included a crash course on the Indian way of life, performing arts traditions, philosophy, history and literature.

A season of recitals in Nepal followed, closing with a memorable drive with M.K. Rasgotra, the Indian ambassador to Nepal, from Kathmandu to Tibet.

We drove on the Araniko highway, passing amazing river gorges and steep mountains. When we reached Tatopani, I plunged into the hot water spring, to the amazement of the protocol officers accompanying us, and swam to my heart's content.

Sonal's performances in India and other countries continued with long breaks in summer and around Christmas, which she spent with Georg and his children at Montreal and with Georg alone at his family home in Aufham, Germany.

It was an old, decrepit place with strong winds that whipped all the trees into weird shapes. There was no central heating. To bathe, we had to use a small tub in the basement, sheltering ourselves from bitter winds. To catch the sun we would go for long drives with sweeping views of the Bavarian lakes or spend a day at the beautiful home of a friend in Dachau—a home with a fantastic collection of artwork and a fruit orchard full of spring flowers.

In Montreal, I enjoyed my role as nanny to Georg's children, Christoph and Claudia. We binged on chocolates, went for walks, discovered new neighbourhoods, shared stories. The children enjoyed watching me dance. We picnicked in parks, gorging on baskets of food. Normal things. Georg continued his wine lessons, teaching me to pick the right German white wines, and to team them up with seafood or slow-cooked bolognese pasta.

Juggling different commitments, Sonal continued with her performing life. She remembers the tumult in her life in the mid-1970s when she had to choose from a maelstrom of competing invitations. She finally accepted a private invitation to perform at different venues in Brazil. To begin with, there were three performances lined up for her at Sao Paulo. The venue was Theatro Municipal, its ornate façade reminiscent of the Palais Garnier of Paris. Not used to the idea of solo performances, the director of Theatro Municipal initially developed cold feet. Ignoring him, on the opening night, Sonal first danced Odissi, beginning with a mangalacharan, graduating to a pallavi composition based on three ragas—Sankarabharnam, Khamaj and Bageshree—distilling their nuances without oversimplifying them. Following the pallavi with an abhinaya piece based on a Radha–Krishna story, Sonal ended the Odissi part of her performance with a moksha. The second part, Bharatanatyam, began with an alarippu and a varnam set to *ragamalika*. She went on to dance to her favourite padam, 'Krishna Nee Begane Baro', and concluded with a tillana performed with an incredible surge of energy. At the end of the recital, the audience erupted. The applause was deafening. A big basket of spring flowers from the director followed Sonal to the green room.

The theatre that was only a quarter full on that momentous opening night was packed to capacity on the third and fourth nights.

The audience went a bit nuts, screaming 'Bravo! Bravo!' There was a doctor who came night after night, delighting in my performances. After my final recital, he came to say goodbye with a baby magnolia tree covered with exquisite flowers. His eyes were moist.

Sonal's audiences followed her even after performances, when she walked through the *fieras* or street markets, asking for her autograph. She was frequently importuned by complete strangers who seemed fascinated by her dress, coiffure, jewellery, her gorgeous luminosity. She made even smoking look chic and sexy and was taken to be the Indian version of Audrey Hepburn and Marlene Dietrich.

Sonal's next destination in Brazil was Salvador de Bahia, where two performances were lined up.

After a searingly intense performance, I drank a glass of their potent, fermented sugarcane liquor, Cachaça, and danced to blaring street music on the cobblestone alleys of the Pelourinho neighbourhood with exuberant locals. My musicians were busy ogling scantily clad women. There were more performances teamed with impromptu street parties at Brasilia and Porto Alegre and Rio where we joined the Cariocas in celebrating the build-up to the soccer match between Argentina and Brazil.

In 1979, Sonal went on an ICCR-supported performance tour of around seventy days to countries across different continents. One of the highlights of this tour was a new choreography based on a famous Malayalam poem, 'Magdalena Mariam', written by Vallathol Narayana Menon (a leading early-twentieth-century Malayalam poet, popularly known as Mahakavi Vallathol). 'Maria Magdalena' was part of her repertory 1975 onwards. Strung to Carnatic ragas and danced in Bharatanatyam, it was a rage in different religious and social contexts. The composition extolled the exquisite beauty of Mary, the *nayika* (or the female protagonist), preparing to meet her lover, her change of heart at the sight of Jesus and her absolute surrender at his feet.

Performed in Brazil, Venezuela, Panama, Mexico and Nicaragua, this composition became a rage across Central and Latin America.

I remember my Mexico experience in vivid detail. I was dancing at the International Cervantino Festival, held in one of Mexico's most colourful and lively cities, Guanajuato. It was an open-air space in a large plaza that could house stadium-sized crowds. I was inundated with felicitations. A group of Mexican peasants wearing sombrero hats also came forward. They had tears in their eyes, and garlic on their breath as they sat on their knees to kiss my hands. Speaking to me in native dialect in voices cracking with emotion, they said that they too saw Jesus as I danced. One of the organizers told me that this group was the loudest in their catcalls during the items preceding this composition.

Performances at Berkeley, Chicago, Washington, New York, London, Paris, Geneva and Moscow were also lined up, some of them at remarkably short notice. She remembers being invited by the Indian embassy in Washington on three days' notice from Mexico. And once she arrived there, she was astounded by the embassy's laid-back approach. She had to clean the performance stage along with her musicians. There was barely any publicity. One of her American fans at the performance told the Washington correspondent of *India Today,*

There's something wrong with your embassy. I mean, a few weeks back, a Ceylon-born writer of successful pornographic novels came to town and the public relations people were able to get her featured in the Style (society) section of the *Washington Post*. But here, your country's Isadora Duncan comes to town and most of us Americans don't even know about it.[3]

Despite her maddening schedule, Sonal took time off to sink her teeth into art-house films, musical soirées and operas.

A complete Wagnerphile, I kept going back to Bayreuth year after year to perform, conduct workshops and feast on operas. I also studied the ballet form by following Paul Taylor, Merce Cunningham and Cuban ballerina and choreographer Alicia Alonso's body of work. I met Maya Plisetskaya, one of the most famous ballerinas of the twentieth century, who stepped into the shoes of Galina Ulanova, in a Bolshoi studio the morning after my Odissi performance at the Bolshoi in 1977. I was mesmerized by her perfect movements and immense life force. Also her blazing red hair! My personal favourite was Marcia Haydée, a Brazilian-born ballet dancer, who took over the direction of the Stuttgart Ballet in 1976. I loved her as Blanche in *A Streetcar Named Desire*.

Sonal's own life was mutating into an inflammatory drama. Always known to be sexually capricious, stories of Georg's sexual liaisons were beginning to unsettle her. In her absence, his apartment in Montreal was cuckooed by young girls. The beginning of the end came when she returned to the apartment unexpectedly one afternoon to find Georg in bed with a Swedish girl with enormous breasts. It was an era where men were often obsessed with breasts, and what she saw that afternoon could have been a scene from Fellini's *Amarcord*. The girl reminded Sonal of Volpino, the nymphomaniac. Something snapped within her. Georg tried to explain, but what her eyes saw was beyond explanation. The year was 1977. Sonal and Georg separated, but their marriage survived a few more years, bridged by a chasm of indifference.

In a revelatory close-up in an interview given to Pritish Nandy in 1984 for a cover story in the *Illustrated Weekly of India*, Sonal said,

Those who married me or loved me, entered the relationship with open eyes. They got to see me as a dancer. They even admired me. But later, they found it difficult to live with someone like me, it was my spirit of freedom, my commitment to dance, that bothered them. A dancer must work very hard, rehearse, be in top physical form all the time. It needs long hours of work and much as you may try to continue it with being a good wife, a good hostess, somehow the equations tend to go awry.[4]

* * *

We are sitting near a large portrait of Sonal painted by M.F. Hussain.

Your choppy personal life must have fuelled gossip. You were caught in the tawdriest of sex scandals. Did you talk about it?

No, for me there was dance first and then everything else. I did have panic attacks when I realized that Georg was cheating. What I saw grossed me out—after that, everything between us was razed to cinders. I can't claim that there were no hard feelings, but I was not interested in tabloid exposés. Seriously, by then I had learnt to square up to the unforeseen betrayals in life. Marriage was certainly not destined to be my stand-in for happiness. I reminded myself of the impermanence of all things, of relationships forming–dissolving.

You were also seen as a bit of an edgy outlier in the early 1970s. Were you looking to shock?

No, but neither was I interested in pretending to be a conformist, or promoting a squeaky-clean image to quieten the chatteratti. My personal life was my own business. The swirl of controversies generated by my live-in relationship with Georg, outrageous stories of my romantic foibles— none of these really bothered me. I certainly did not counter them!

You were the cynosure of all eyes. How did you cope with so much adulation?

I must confess I was a little startled at being at the centre stage of so much attention. Every time I gave a good performance, I would wait for the shears to come out. Nowadays, during a live performance you see hundreds of digital lenses raised to record the events, but in the good old days it was more of a shared excitement, with little emotional distance between the performer and the audience, even media. The cameras would explode into life at different points, but not in an intimidating way.

Some of the adulation stays with you. When I danced at the Bolshoi, for instance, a star-struck young reporter from one of Moscow's leading newspapers wrote an ode to my little red shoes, which were actually my feet smeared with *alta*, the red dye commonly used by dancers.

You loved baiting your critics and admirers, didn't you? Let's look at your conversation with Shobhaa De in the *Express* magazine. She called you the undisputed prima donna of Delhi. Replying to her question on what you enjoyed most, you said, 'A good swim. A good cigar. A good . . .' Wasn't that provocative? Incendiary?

Seditious, subversive . . . *(laughs uproariously)*

You have been far from apolitical. How did you deal with a period as dark as the Emergency? Did you join any of the underground movements?

The violation of key constitutional rights during the Emergency outraged me. It felt as if the country was disembowelling itself. Poets I admired, like Girdhar Rathi and Baba Nagarjun, were in jail. Film-makers like Anand Patwardhan were underground. Phanishwar Nath Renu[5] and Shivaram Karanth[6] returned their Padma awards. There was a significant spread of quiet dissent through street theatre. There was Safdar Hashmi's Jana Natya Manch (JANAM),[7] and artists like Gulam Mohammed Sheikh,

Gieve Patel and Vivan Sundaram were radicalizing cultural spaces through their work. So, in a sense, fear was balanced by acts of resistance.

In Karnataka, one of our socialist friends, C.G.K. Reddy, used the traditional form of storytelling, the yakshagana,[8] to comment on contemporary political issues. But I must confess that in Delhi, with the political climate getting insanely paranoid, most of us were shut in our personal silos. I refused offers to dance at a couple of events organized by the government.

For me, the crackdown on free thought was a period of intense inner churning. My closest friends were poster boys of resistance. Many of them were detained under MISA[9] and tortured. For instance, George Fernandes and Viren Shah were implicated falsely in the Baroda Dynamite Conspiracy and arrested in June 1976 in Calcutta. Another friend, Madhu Limaye, was detained under MISA from July 1975 to February 1977, in different jails. They were tortured, but their spirit remained unbroken. It was a carnival of resistance.

Did you celebrate when it ended?

Yes, we celebrated the unbroken spirit. It was also beginning of a period of introspection and of a deeper, direct engagement with politics.

You were part of a socialist group . . .

Yes, we were called the young socialist gang/brigade. There was George Fernandes with his coxcomb of tousled hair.

There was Madhu Dandavate with his polite reticence. And my dear friend Madhu Limaye, elected four times to the Lok Sabha from 1964 to 1979, an encyclopedia when it came to the Indian Constitution. I remember visiting his little flat on Pandara Road when he was elected general secretary of the Janata Party on 1 May 1977, which was also his birthday. 'Madhu, your girlfriend is here,' announced his wife, Champa, lovingly. Madhuji went to the kitchen and made some delicious kheer and khichri for a group of us celebrating there that night. We had a raucous time! We made George execute dizzying spins. There was something immensely funny and cartoony when he spun around waving his hands clumsily. We laughed our heads off.

Madhuji had an irrepressible appetite for classical music. I remember going to the Shankar Lal Hall with him and Champa to listen to the last *jugalbandi*[10] of Ali Akbar Khan and Ravi Shankar. Alla Rakha was on the tabla as an accompanist, soloist and sparring partner. We went to several concerts together.

Who were your other friends?

Mercurial, mischievous Mani Shankar of a somewhat wily, indefatigable intellect. Jasleen Dhamija and Veena Shroff, with whom I had a soul-baring friendship. Ramakrishna Hegde, a *rasik*,[11] who embellished his stories with the most entertaining anecdotes, and his wife, Shaku. Salman and Kusum Haider who I knew from my Kabul days. There were Prakash Shah and Vinu, O.P. Jain, Satish and Kiran

Gujral, Vasant Sathe and N.K.P. Salve. And then there was Vajpayeeji, ebullient and warm with a ready smile, his voice a spacey drawl. Even when he was prime minister, his affection for me did not burn out. He would find time to slip into my recitals, he would come home for quiet evenings. Sometimes even the banality of our conversation would make the evening special.

He was known as an astute politician, a good orator, a writer poet, but what about his overwhelming generosity? I remember getting a taste of that when I was taking my production, *Draupadi*, to the Melbourne Theatre Festival where I had been invited to perform. The year was 1998. The trouble was that I was completely broke at that point and had no money to buy an air ticket for my stage manager. A chance meeting with Vajpayeeji sorted things out. He called me over for a discussion unexpectedly one afternoon, in his office space at 7, Safdarjung Road. Brushing past his SPG guards[12] and Shiv Kumar, his burly aide, I went in to see him. Once the discussion was over, I narrated my woes to him over a glass of masala coke. Vajpayeeji was playing with his dogs, Sassy and Sophie. He got up and went to an almirah and surfaced with a weathered wallet. Without any fanfare, he handed over the money for my manager's air ticket!

Were there any romantic misadventures?

No, these were sweet, uncomplicated friendships. Some of my male friends did have a penchant for horseplay but never took liberties with me.

You were courted by many attractive men, resulting in uncomfortable brushes with back-page gossip.

Who cares about some tittle-tattle?

What about your friendship with Muhammad Yunus? He was in the inner circle of someone you considered a despot. And yet you were friends. It was rumoured that he called you his 'bulbul'.

Yes, there was a contradiction. But we became friends in 1972, much before he became a special envoy of Mrs Gandhi in 1975. When I was homeless, a period of intense anxiety, he kept my luggage in his garage. When I hired a house, he would visit often.

And tell you not to tell Mrs Gandhi?

Yes, always (*laughs*). Indira Gandhi, whatever her faults, used to love artists. I was invited to accompany her thrice as part of cultural delegations abroad. She also invited me home. In the warmth of her home, we talked about taking India's cultural heritage forward.

10

Pulling Back the Curtains

If parts of the 1970s were shadowed with pain and turbulence, the remaining years were marked by a whirlwind of joyful engagements. Sonal decided that Delhi would be her home.

I have always looked beyond the city's clichés. Delhi is a much mocked city, but I am in love with it.

She moved into C-304, a rented house in Delhi's Defence Colony. Though small, it had a classy, vintage feel.

Even though it was a rented house, this was a space I could truly call my home. A space where I could dream, create, teach, love and plan my itinerary. The words of a famous Uruguayan litterateur[1] danced in my head when I went about buying new plates, cushions, rugs: 'There is no doubt, this is my house . . . I occur here, I deceive myself greatly here . . . This is my house detained in time.'

Sonal started teaching in 1976, worn out by the perseverance of Swati,[2] her first student. At the point at which sixteen-year-old Swati came into her life, she felt her energy was being leeched away by various commitments. But Swati was a fireball of quiet determination.

> She stood outside my door for three to four months, alone, on her ride back from college, and sometimes with her anxious-looking mother. I said, 'Don't bug me, please, I don't teach.' I also put difficult conditions to put her off—you'll have to come any time I ask you to, you'll be able to leave only when I permit . . . Swati, however, did not budge.
>
> I was ruthless with her, mocked her when she could not bend for armandi. I used to laugh seeing her walk like a duck because of intense pain, but she persevered. After a while, I too realized that passion for dance must be nurtured and supported. She is a celebrated Bharatanatyam dancer now and runs a dance foundation in New York. Other students followed—Meera Krishna, Pallavi Sethi, Pallavi Saran, Rita Sharma, Pranita Bhandari, Ketaki Kumar, Shantanu, Dr Pramod Kohli, Vanshica Kant.

It was Sonal's Congress friend, Vasant Sathe,[3] who motivated her to establish the Centre for Indian Classical Dances (CICD) to nourish the art sensitivity of young students and to ensure that classical dances do not wither away. In his words, 'Over the years, I saw Sonal develop into a scholarly exponent of Indian classical dances and thought she would be the best person to establish a centre for the serious study and propagation of Indian dance styles.' A little reluctant initially, Sonal was persuaded by her friends, Narendra Salve, Madhu Limaye and Veena Shroff, to consider the idea seriously. It did not take long for her to be gripped by the exhilarating possibility of creating a space that would be a Mecca for aspiring classical dance students.

The centre was registered on 30 April 1977, Sonal's thirty-third birthday. It moved to its present permanent location in Gulmohar Institutional Area in 2001—a spacious, elegant building with contemporary design sensibilities. For several years, the centre operated from her home.

> There was very little space. Every afternoon before the classes, we moved the living room furniture to make space for my students. Sometimes I held classes in the austere setting of my garage—but despite the ad-hocism, the number of my students kept growing.

Even though it operated modestly for a long time, Sonal's Centre for Indian Classical Dances was built with a strong, uncompromising vision of what an institution for teaching and propagation of Indian classical performing arts traditions should be. The method of teaching then and now is based on pedagogic experience of the guru–shishya parampara. Fundamentally, this ensures that the shishya or student imbibes the aesthetic values of his/her teacher's or guru's artistic lineage.

> I try to bring the knowledge and wisdom of my gurus to my dance studio, but I also realize how much has changed. As a dance student, I was told to imbibe five vital attributes of a *sadhak* or student—of a crow who is frugal about

the time taken to bathe; of an egret or crane that stands in single-minded concentration on one leg to catch fish; of a dog who sleeps lightly; one who eats sparingly; and finally one who is ready to give up everything in search of knowledge. It is true that dance needs absolute immersion, but I can't expect my students to be sequestered in their dance world. Hence, even though I walk the fine line between tradition and modernity, I don't compromise on rigour and discipline.

Joining as awkward beginners, students at the centre start with yoga to get over the limitation and constraints of the body, sitting shoeless and cross-legged in their maroon-and-yellow salwar–kameez–dupatta uniforms.

Dance is actually yoga, dynamic yoga, and must follow the rules of slow warm-up, and regular and controlled practice. The simplest of adavus requires initial training of at least six months of yogasanas.

Once this is done, a structured curriculum of training in Bharatanatyam and Odissi in initiated. A working knowledge of Indian music, iconography, temple sculptures and paintings too is part of the curriculum. Sonal has also made lessons in Sanskrit mandatory.

You may think I am schoolmarmish, but I insist on my students learning Sanskrit shlokas and regurgitating them in class. Respect for their cultural heritage and for the arts is a must.

One of the stories I narrate to the beginners is of the dialogue between King Vajra and Markandeya in the famous Indian text, *Visnudharmottara Purana*. King Vajra requests the sage to accept him as his disciple and teach him the art of making icons, so he might worship the deities in their proper forms. The sage replies that it is not possible to comprehend the rudiments of image-making without the knowledge of painting. The king wishes to learn painting but is told that unless he is accomplished as a dancer, he cannot grasp the basics of painting. The king requests that he be taught dance, whereupon the sage replies that, without a sense of rhythm or knowledge of music, proficiency in dance would be a pipe dream. Dance, as a matter of fact, is a complete art form. It enfolds sculpture, painting, music, drama and poetry.

When Sonal teaches, there is nothing starry or divaesque about her. Her students, a close, tight-knit group, are incredibly under her spell.

When they join my classes, I am gobsmacked by how little they know. But slowly, over a few weeks, a change occurs. They begin to enjoy the exuberance of dance. I relax and allow myself to exult in their performances.

In 1977–78, Sonal was fizzing with ideas that were not all froth. The seeds sown at a dhrupad concert at the Brooklyn Academy of Music resulted in the formation of SPICMACAY (Society for the Promotion of Indian Classical Music and Culture Amongst Youth), an avant-garde, classical, pop-up arts movement for young people. Initiated by Dr Kiran Seth, an IIT alumnus, the movement was strongly supported by the younger Dagar brothers[4] and Sonal. Working on an idea originally proposed by Sonal, the first lec-dem series was held in 1979 when six artists—Sonal, Asad Ali Khan, the Dagar brothers, Munawar Ali Khan and Pandit Birju Maharaj gave lec-dems at the Godavari Hostel of the Jawaharlal Nehru University in Delhi, in the presence of Justice Y.V. Chandrachud, the then chief justice of India. Lec-dems in other Delhi colleges like Lady Irwin College and Miranda House followed. Many other artists like Pandit Jasraj, Dr T.N. Krishnan, Lalgudi Jayaraman, Hariprasad Chaurasia, Shivkumar Sharma and Amjad Ali Khan joined the movement, lending it gravitas, passion and commitment. In 1982, the first lec-dem series in schools was conducted in Delhi. Zia Mohiuddin Dagar, Amjad Ali Khan and Sonal pioneered the initiative at Modern School, Sardar Patel Vidyalaya and Ramjas School.

> We took the movement to schools and colleges at distant places to extend its outreach. I remember spending several nights in venues that were inaccessible, in mosquito-ridden, shabby rooms with peeling plasters and dirty linen, using public transport, performing for a pittance, putting in our own resources to keep the movement alive and vibrant. Braving the winter chill, young art aficionados would come wrapped in heavy shawls and blankets for our lecture-demonstrations. We had to deal with bad lighting, poor sound systems. Sometimes there was not even a *pandal*—we would perform under a canopy of stars, giving impromptu

tweaks to the most standard of repertories. Even the uninitiated would stand around watching and listening attentively.

Sonal's lec-dems and solo performances continued. If due to shoestring budgets she couldn't take musicians along, she danced to taped music. She also introduced the lec-dem format in the cultural spaces of the India International Centre at Delhi. This happened at the behest of John Lall, the director of the India International Centre in the mid-1970s. 'Leading dancers came and shared their understanding of their dance form, and encouraged participants to copy a few simple steps.' Her association with cultural events at the India International Centre continued with successive directors like Uma Shankar Bajpai, Eric Gonzalves and A. Madhavan, but became tenuous thereafter.

Sonal thought she was done with long-term relationships after separating from Georg Lechner, when she met Narendra Singh Bhati at the Jodhpur airport in 1977. She had arrived in Jodhpur en route to Jaisalmer to attend a royal wedding when she saw a man with a Salvadore Dali-like moustache reaching out to her at the tarmac. In his Jodhpuri breeches he looked like he had just finished riding or playing polo. That was Narendra, sent there to receive her by Jujhar Singh, the state tourism minister.

Sonal and Narendra developed a raw intimacy that unravelled slowly.

Jodhpur, the city, worked its spell on me. Call me a diehard romantic, but spending time with him in the romantic setting of one of its prettiest heritage hotels, with fairy lights cascading from the roof and treetops, I was consumed by dreams of romantic love.

After a long time, Sonal was in a happy personal space. Narendra Singh Bhati was a music and dance aesthete. His literary and poetic sensibilities matched hers. He shared her appetite for travel and adventure. He smothered her with endearments. In all senses, it was a charming, adrenaline-packed romance.

Despite the fact that Bhati was close to the Nehru–Gandhi family, even my socialist friends embraced him fully. The gathering in my spartan new home would swell to a small salon whenever he visited. There were a number of expat friends who would also pop in.

Prominent amongst Sonal's expat friends at the time were Peter Curtis, the Australian high commissioner to India, and his wife Chantal; Heinrich Rauffer, a classmate of Georg Lechner who continued to host her during summer festivals in Germany even after her divorce; the US ambassador, Dr Robert Goheen, and his wife Margaret. Dr Goheen was the president of Princeton University till 1972. He returned there in 1981 as a senior fellow at the Woodrow Wilson School. Sonal spent memorable vacations at his home in Princeton. Another friend was the well-known Venezuelan author and diplomat, Frank Bracho, someone whom Hugo Chavez greatly admired.

Over the years Sonal's Centre for Indian Classical Dances became the focal point of many activities. A festival of dance and music was part of the yearly calendar. Sonal's Bharatanatyam and Urmila Nagar's Kathak, Hariprasad Chaurasia's flute and

Kishori Amonkar's vocals marked the first of these events in 1977. In September, Sonal danced in aid of the Flood Relief Fund. The following year, the Krishna legend in classical dance was showcased by acclaimed dancers, Uma Sharma, Sanjukta Panigrahi, Raja and Radha Reddy, dancers from the International Centre for Kathakali and the Natya Ballet Centre, and Sonal. A festival showcasing the performing arts tradition of Orissa followed, and so it went on year after year.

The festivals were mounted on a modest scale with the exception of the exposition on the Krishna legend held in May 1978, which was inaugurated by Morarji Desai, the then prime minister. In his address, Morarji Desai confessed that he was there in his personal capacity as my kaka, not as prime minister. The run-up to his presence at the exposition was quite funny. My father called me up sometime in 1977 and asked me to visit Morarji kaka. The latter had complained to my grandfather that I had not visited him even once ever since he became prime minister.

When I saw him, he asked me if I was still indulging in my passion for dance. I was stung. I called him Aurangzeb and tried to whip up an argument. I asked him why no artist, especially a woman artist, had been deemed fit for the highest office of the President of India. I remember taking two names in support of my argument—M.S. Subbulakshmi and Rukmini Devi Arundale. Kaka listened patiently end eventually did offer Rukmini Devi the presidency. She declined, choosing dance over presidency. Kaka's gesture, however, endeared him to me and I asked him to be our chief guest. He watched the entire performance in a sombre, reflective mood, nodding at me approvingly after my recital.

Sonal started the tradition of organizing dance-appreciation courses. In December 1981, a six-day course was conducted for Kuchipudi, Manipuri and Kathakali dances by leading danseuses like Vempati Chinna Satyam, Singhajit Singh and Sadanand Balakrishna. Two years later, Sonal joined Jiwan Pani and Mayadhar Raut to conduct a course on Odissi, and in 1984, she invited her gurus U.S. Krishna Rao, Chandrabhaga Devi and Jayalakshmi Alva to conduct an appreciation programme on Bharatanatyam.

The Centre for Indian Classical Dances gradually began to work as a think tank and forum for presentation of interdisciplinary research in dance history, theory and music, attracting scholars of dance studies and those involved in the practice of dance. Seminars on Odissi abhinaya, the role of nattuvanars, Odissi music, *Geet Govind* and the *Natyashastra* attracted participants from a range of backgrounds.

At the CICD, the research unit was led by Jiwan Pani, Sonal's trusted mentor, who was also by now her rakhi[5]-brother. Her own abiding research interest in the music of *Geet Govind* led them to research the thirteenth-century text, *Sangeet Ratnakar*. They discovered in its rich text the entire raga and tala repertory used in the *Geet Govind*. Bankim Sethi, who was part of the research team, recalls, 'We researched, had long discussions. Sonal respected our views, encouraged us to think out of the box.' The music of *Geet Govind* also became the subject of an important seminar held by the CICD. It was attended by eminent scholars, musicians and musicologists like Dr Sumati Mutatkar, Dr Nilamadhab Panigrahi, Radha Krishnamurthy, Pandit Markandeya Mohapatra, Pandit Kashinath Pujapanda and Bankim Sethi. The ashtapadis sung in ragas Vasant and Shri from *Sangeet Ratnakar* took everyone's breath away.

Research in a particular area was also sometimes prompted by her audience. For instance, during a lec-dem in a college campus in Trichur, Sonal was stumped by a seemingly innocuous question from a young woman. 'Why do compositions on which you dance and sing always refer to the male god as "beloved" or "lover"? What about goddesses? Is there anywhere that a goddess in thus addressed by a male poet?' Days of intense research followed. Finally, Jiwan da found the answer in *Chariya Geeti* of the Buddhist Tantric texts and Sonal chose two songs that have a female *aaradhya*.[6]

Sonal's favourite geeti is 'Shoonya Mahari',[7] a dialogue between Sabari, a tribal woman symbolizing life energy, and Sabara, a young man symbolizing the body. Her most memorable performance of 'Shoonya Mahari' was before the Dalai Lama at the Tibetan Institute of Performing Arts at Dharamsala.

I was on stage after my performance to receive blessings from His Holiness. He came up, hugged me tightly and asked in a choked voice, 'How could you guess that Sabari is my *kuladevi* [the primary deity of his clan]?'

The moments preceding my performance were no less memorable. When I arrived at the institute, my neck was blessed with the flowing white silk scarf that His Holiness the Dalai Lama had draped a few minutes ago. Thousands jostled to peer at me, wave and nod at me with knowing

smiles. At the gate of the institute, the director, faculty
and other functionaries greeted me profusely, touching the
ground in front, thanking me with moist eyes, folding hands
in namaskar. I could not for the life of me comprehend
these 'thanks' even before the recital was performed, since it
is always done after! Recognizing my confusion, my escort
serenely explained on way to the green room that they were
thankful to me for bringing His Holiness to the institute
for the first time and that my visit to Dharamsala and
giving a special dance programme was responsible for their
precincts to be hallowed by His Holiness's presence. My
eyes brimmed over. Such intense love! Such unconditional
devotion! Such deep faith![8]

The relentless churning during this period led to the
recontextualization of Sonal's choreographies. She began to
question the notion that the performing arts leave one a little
apolitical, a little disengaged. A dancer is not just a dancer. She
is a part of this environment. She does not exist in a vacuum.
A society and its happenings have an impact on all individuals,
especially artists. If an art form does not reflect existing milieu,
it stagnates. Playful and inventive, she began using the leitmotif
in historical classical texts to explore contemporary meanings
without undermining dance aesthetics.

Sonal's choreographies went into overdrive. Writing
about the process of rollout of original compositions and
choreographies, Sonal reminisces,

It had been my habit to write down my thoughts which
inspired me to work. Sometimes it took them years before

being translated into actual choreography, also perhaps because of my predilection for composing original music too. From early years I was very particular that music should be visual, i.e. listening to music, one should be able to visualize dance and understand the storyline. The mood and situation of the character should reflect in music. Then too, my insistence on getting at not just word-meaning but meaning with nuances and *dhwani* (unexpressed meaning) would guide me through meandering texts, subtexts and commentaries with my scholar friends who enjoyed endless hours of debate and discussion with me.[9]

She continued to work with Bankim, bringing the undeniable chemistry of his music and her dance into her productions. There was a line-up of spectacular productions, operatic in scale—ranging from *Mary Magdalene*, *Meghdootam*, *Ritu Samhara*, *Kumar Sambhavam*, *Amrit Manthan*, *Radhayani*, *Sudama Charita* and *Geet Govind*—moving her dance into the category of classical dance-theatre, shaped by an unusual dramatic intensity.

Every time I planned a new choreography, taking inspiration from one of our great scholarly texts, my brain gave me a good fix of dopamine.

She toured her productions with a live ensemble of musicians. Sonal broke the celebrity bubble when she took her productions out of the confines of structured, tiered spaces and big-budget extravaganzas. In 1988, her production, *Sudama Charita*, was performed in eight different locations in Delhi alone—from an open-air stage in the Central Park at Connaught Place to non-theatrical locations in the slums of Shahdara, Geeta Colony, Nangloi and Chirag Dilli.

I received some support from the North Zone Cultural Centre, but had to essentially work on a shoestring budget. Hundreds of men, women and children would stream into the festive pandals. There seemed to be a genuine hunger and need for experiencing classical art forms. I don't remember a single occasion when there was mayhem. I felt a way through their thoughts and expectations and levitated with joy when I was told that I had sown creative seeds in artistically arid grounds.

Sonal's romance with Narendra Singh Bhati continued to be exciting, bordering on the turbulent, much like a white-water ride.

His political commitments[10] and the pressures of my sixty-hour workweeks notwithstanding, we managed to have a blast travelling through different parts of Rajasthan in his little black fiat, followed sometimes by Peter and Chantal's ambassadorial Mercedes. We thought nothing of spending hours in the relentless heat of the desert if the fan belt of our car broke. We spent nights in tents lit by kerosene lamps in luxury resorts to listen to the haunting songs of the Langas and Manganiars,[11] the sound of their dholaks and wooden clappers following us as we left the desert.

As tourism minister of Rajasthan, Narendra started a chain of roadside eateries called Midway, where we would stop to eat huge, slap-on meals. When Narendra started the luxury train, Palace on Wheels, in 1983, I designed the logo and selected the crockery. I helped refurbish Jogi Mahal, located inside the Ranthambore National Park. There were trips to London, to Geneva, Zurich and my favourite city Paris, dining on the Seine in the boat Bateaux Mouches, looking at the illuminated riverside, walking on the cobbled lane in Montmartre, meeting friends at the historic brasserie, La Coupole, evenings at the Cinémathèque or at an opera. What a time! I was like a teenager, moving through extremes of ecstasy and anguish in this relationship, tears after a bitter fight, followed by incessant joyful laughter.

Sonal continued with her Bharatanatyam and Odissi recitals, juxtaposing them to create *Dwi-varana*, a solo choreography. The 1980s passed in a blur of performances, averaging fifty to sixty annually, in India and abroad. The season began with performances at the Akademie der Künste[12] in Berlin, one of the oldest cultural institutes in Europe. She was accompanied by Thanil Singh, a young Manipuri dancer whose performance incorporated the vigorous beating of a double-headed drum in a dance known as *Pung Cholom*.

It was a double stage, one for dancers and another at a little lower level for musicians. While beating his drum with acrobatic body movements, Thanil fell on the lower stage. I improvised and danced around him. The audience could not see through the improvisation.

When she was not dancing, her evenings were spent in Berlin's opera houses seeing great performances, and at the

Philharmonic, home to the Berlin Philharmoniker, seeing the legendary Herbert von Karajan lead the orchestra.

Sonal danced at different places in Germany nearly every successive year, the only constant being Bayreuth where she continued to hold workshops. There were invitations to perform in China, the Philippines, Australia, Switzerland, Italy, the USA, the Netherlands, Bulgaria, Czechoslovakia and at the picturesque setting of the Algarve festival in Portugal. In all these places, she made an unforgettable impression. 'Her mere presence compels attention so that whether she is performing her art or describing it in words, she is a most persuasive ambassador for Indian dance,' wrote Alan Brissenden, an Australian art critic, after a performance. He further said, 'Sonal Mansingh is one of those rare artists who combine a joyous personality with a flawless technique.'

In 1983, she went on a Southeast Asia dance tour with recitals spread over different venues in Indonesia, Laos, Vietnam, Cambodia, Hong Kong and South Korea. Her troupe of eight musicians went with her.

Sometimes the local arrangements were of a very poor order. For instance, in Laos, I was made to stay in a crumbling, ramshackle, old guest house on a frangipani-lined street. But my performance at the festival of Boun That Luang more than made up for it. I danced under the full moon at the sacred golden stupa. Thousands of monks attended my performance along with locals and tourists. People came carrying incense sticks and candles as offerings.

Another poignant memory is related to Phnom Penh, Cambodia, where she saw the remains of decades of war and genocide. Cramped in one of the three surviving planes of Pol Pot's regime and escorted by the military police, she arrived at the barbed-wire Tuol Sleng prison, formerly a school, transformed by Khmer Rouge into an interrogation centre, and heard stories of unbelievable torture. She was taken to Choeung Ek, one of the notorious killing fields where prisoners were taken for execution. She tried to block out the experience by focusing on the stupendous temples of Angkor Vat in Siem Reap and her acclaimed performances at the National Theatre.

On her last morning in Siem Reap, she was taken to the Royal Palace museum complex to see a performance by the Royal Kampuchean Ballet.

Thousands of Buddhas of silver, gold, diamond, sapphire and emerald sat in meditation, untouched by glory or tragedy. I sat in a pavilion with mosaic floors where around eighty young girls and boys danced and chanted verses. Teenage girls danced the apsara dance, their innocent faces radiating with beatific smiles. Young boys in frayed trousers danced with joyous abandon.

I was overcome with bliss, but not for long. I was informed that each of the dancers was an orphan, survivor of the atrocities of Khmer Rouge. I was introduced to three surviving teachers of the once hundred-strong Royal Kampuchean Ballet contingent. I was completely numb with sorrow. The fiery, burnt orange sun spilling over the Mekong river that afternoon seemed like a cruel reminder of all this country had gone through. I sift through my Cambodia memories constantly. They have added to the strength of my dance narratives.

And then there are city-memories and food-memories. In the city of Ho Chi Minh in Vietnam, Sonal danced at the Opera House located in the heart of the city, and ate plump bowls of rice noodles with smoked fish at a lavish banquet-spread that night. She also spent joyous times in Hanoi where everyone was very friendly and wanted to dance with her as she walked in the old quarter with its labyrinth of motorbike-clogged streets, catching a performance of water-puppetry by the Hoàn Kiêm lake.

Sipping endless passion fruit and yoghurt smoothies, surrounded by cheerful fans, it was difficult to think of Vietnam as a country bombed by the Americans, and poisoned with Agent Orange.

In her collage of memories, Sonal reserves a special place to memories linked with Tikki Kaul, one of India's foremost diplomats. He occupied a ringside seat during three very different Soviet regimes, headed by Stalin, Brezhnev and Gorbachev.

I visited the Soviet Union in the summer of 1988 to perform at Murmansk, the world's largest city north of the Arctic Circle. Tikki Kaul, then the Indian ambassador with a cabinet rank, came to Murmansk to watch me perform along with the then information counsellor, Veena Sikri.

Tikki introduced me in Russian to the audience in superlative terms and watched over my performance like a hawk. His hilarious Russian anecdotes during the cocktail reception that followed completely enthralled me. I remember going back to the hotel well past 10 p.m. It was a polar day with bright sunshine even at that hour. Early morning was like a winter morning with piercing winds, but by afternoon, spring was in the air. I saw the most incredible polar poppies part-hidden in lichen and white sheets of snow, a metaphor for a country crawling towards light, openness and glasnost.

Sonal continued to perform in different festivals in India, at Khajuraho, Kalakshetra, Rajgir, Badrinath, Brihadeeswara, Gangasagar, Modhera, Sankat Mochan, Bhagyachandra, Sharad Vaibhav, at different Sangeet Natak Akedemi festivals criss-crossing the country and several other places. Many of her performances had inadvertent 'fun' moments.

I was invited to the Badrinath Festival in 1983, in the month of May. Badrinath[13] is known as the second Vaikunth or abode of Lord Vishnu. I performed at noon, much before the early evening *aarti*, to an audience consisting largely of sadhus and devout Hindus who I was sure were familiar with the thousand names of Vishnu recorded in the *Vishnu Sahasranama*.[14] The central piece of my choreography was sixteen names[15] with sixteen attributes that are commonly invoked. These were set in ragamalika, a garland of sixteen ragas set to different rhythmic cycles. I was lost in my dance, but my musicians were greatly amused at the sight of sadhus taking copious notes.

In 1985, my students and I were staging *Amrit Manthan*, when one of the dancers performing the role of an *asura*[16] was struck by a real arrow of love when he saw the apsara Rambha, his current flame, on stage. He got into an amorous mood, caught her hand and began dancing with her. We had to creatively manoeuvre him back to his team of asuras, much to the delight of the audience who saw it as a cleverly contrived moment of comic relief in an otherwise serious production.

The 1980s were also crowded with official felicitations and awards, beginning with the Medal of Friendship presented by the Government of Vietnam in 1983. This was followed by three Indian awards in 1985, Nritya Choodamani, Natya Kala Ratna and the Sahitya Kala Parishad award. In 1986, she was given the Nrityakala Kaumudi award by the government of Andhra Pradesh and the Sangeet Natak Akademi award by the government of Gujarat. The prestigious Sangeet Natak Akademi award came to her a year later, followed by the Shiromani Bhai Veer Singh and Vishwa Gurjari awards in 1989.

Not less than an award was the thrill Sonal experienced when the renowned art maestro, M.F. Hussain, painted her portrait. Sonal was in Pune, in 1988 or 1989, at the time of the Pune Festival, when she met Hussain at a dinner.

I was wearing a peach-and-powder-pink georgette saree. He probably liked my colour palette. While I was sipping my drink, he took out some crayons from one of the pockets of his frayed trousers and started sketching. Rahul Bajaj, who was present there and whom I know well, bought the artwork once it was completed and despatched it to me.

On the face of it, Sonal led a blessed existence, but by the middle of the 1980s, her relationship with Narendra Singh Bhati was turning volatile, prefiguring the dissonance that would claim it later. In a certain sense, her long-running romance contained elements of destruction form the time it started. Despite sharing common interests, the two were hopelessly mismatched. Narendra's politics-fuelled life was driven by extravagant ambition. He began drinking heavily, following the familiar alcoholic cycle of moroseness, destructiveness, self-reproach. Over the years, his alcoholism worsened and took manic proportions.

> I tried to ignore his quirks and flaws for many years, but could not eventually keep up with his alcohol-saturated, out-of-control life. It was tearing down my self-esteem, draining my positive energy.

Often at one another's throats, by 1988–89 she had decided to call it quits. Narendra died in September 2010 of liver-related complications—ravaged by years of drinking. He was sixty-six.

* * *

End of another relationship. How difficult was it to fold the experience and put it aside?

> Not easy. I tried to get away several times before I finally did, but every time felt an undertow of emotions drawing me back. I still spend moments reminiscing about my days with him. A romantic song is often a reminder of the magic of the moments spent together, their emotional heft.

The death of this relationship too must have led to the usual dose of speculation and gossip.

Yes, I fought the agony of another break-up and dealt with all that followed. But friends helped. Madhu Limaye, Veena Shroff, George Fernandes—they all stood by me when I was teetering on the edge. Most of all, spending time with my students helped. With many of them I share a really close bond. And finally, my ability to laugh at myself even when I am wallowing in grief helped too.

You have never luxuriated in your bell jar. At this point you were also teaching. How important is dance education?

Extremely. Dance stimulates all the senses, promotes the development of multisensory beings. Remembering the text, the music and the steps of the vast repertory that dance students learn is not easy. It needs mental dexterity, the ability to absorb and hold information. Research has proven that the textural richness of dance helps in creative problem-solving and encourages students to think outside the box. They learn to love the plurality of cultural traditions. Even particle physics takes inspiration from dance.

Martha Graham called dance the hidden language of the soul. Even though all my students go through the same rigour, each student's artistry ends up being radically different from the other.

Several parents have come to me at different points to tell me about the impact dance has had on their young one's life and on them. For every child, access to dance is vital.

How serious are your students? Do they respect the guru–shishya parampara?

Paramparas also change over time. The traditional gurukul learning experience was very different. It involved the complete sublimation of the student's ego, a complete immersion in the teaching process. I often mourn the death of the rigour of the parampara and wish I could turn the clock back.

One of my favourite stories goes back to the training period of my guru, Prof. Rao, his wife, Chandrabhaga Devi, and their friend Ram Gopal, another acclaimed dancer, who was one of the pioneers of Indian dance in the West. They trained under one of the greatest teachers of Bharatanatyam, Meenakshisundaram Pillai. My gurus and Ramgopal practised daily under the supervision of the great guru in the courtyard of the famous Brihadeeswara temple in Thanjavur. Taking advantage of the great guru's poor eyesight, Ram Gopal decided to play a prank. But the guru's sharp senses sensed there was something wrong. He was incensed.

Seeing him possessed by rage, Ram Gopal and Chandrabhaga Devi took refuge behind a sculptured pillar and a sheepish Krishna Rao alone faced the guru's wrath. Punishment was meted out. Thirty minutes of *sarka*-adavu, a non-stop movement of sitting on the toes, heels joined together, legs stretching out in an elongated movement, with corresponding hand and torso movements. Poor Krishna Rao performed the agonizing feat for what seemed to be an eternity. I too am a strict disciplinarian. Impudent students get a kick up the arse, but not physically.

Getting back to your question about the seriousness of my students, there are a few who, like me, breathe dance in and out like oxygen and for whom dance is a commitment for a lifetime. When I work on group choreographies with them, I am astounded by their creativity and take their suggestions on costumes, lighting and props seriously. Our dance space turns into a shared experience, a communal joy. They ask me questions, they confide in me. They learn to deal with my flashes of temper. We are sometimes seized by uncontrollable laughter. I know all my students intimately. They too know my positive as well as my dark side. If some of my students have for some reason left dance behind, when asked, they will tell you how dance has changed their lives.

Can one learn the rudiments of Indian classical dance by watching it on YouTube?

Only the rudiments. YouTube cannot produce talent that can be taken seriously. Classical dances not only follow a structured, rule-based form, but also necessitate a complex and extremely nuanced interplay between mind and body. They need exceptional musicality. You can't find your way without the personal attention of a guru. You can see demos of different styles on YouTube, learn Bollywood-style dance movements, hip-hop, salsa, zumba. There are also dance video games like 'Just Dance' which encourage you to boogie by matching your movements with the dancer on the screen, but learning classical dances is serious business. You have to fall deeply in love with it. It has to consume you fully. You have to be at the edge of madness.

What would be the appropriate age to start learning dance?

I started when I was seven. Rukmini Devi started at twenty-eight. Ideally, it should be when a child is seven or eight, when the bones are in the process of becoming strong, and the mind starts being receptive.

11

The Personal and the Political

The 1990s began with Sonal's involvement with a group of performing artists, writers and poets, collectively known as 'Artists against Communalism',[1] who worked to uphold the values of secularism and cultural pluralism by bringing together on the same platform the enormous richness of India's classical music and dance traditions. Braving Delhi's winter chill, on 1 January 1991, she joined the group for a sit-in at Delhi's Safdar Hashmi Marg.

The night was dusted with magic. Initially planned for twelve hours, the sit-in stretched for seventeen hours, with an impressive line-up of performers of different genres of art. The participants included Bhisham Sahni, Habib Tanvir, Rahi Masoom Raza, Ali Sardar Jafri, Javed Akhtar, J. Swaminathan, Manjit Bawa, Indrani Rahman, Arpana Caur, Jatin Das, Vivan Sundaram, M.K. Raina, Yamini Krishnamurthy, Birju Maharaj, Krishen Khanna, Ghulam Sheikh, Amjad Ali Khan, Arpita Singh, Paramjeet Singh, Shanti Hiranand, Shubha Mudgal, Asad Ali Khan, Rajan and Sajan Mishra,

Hari Prasad Chaurasia, Dagar Bandhus, the Wadali brothers, Kiran Segal, Madhup Mudgal, Bansi Kaul and many others. Organized by the Safdar Hashmi Memorial Trust, it was an intense experience, stunningly avant garde, with an alchemy of revolutionary music, dance, poetry and prose, crackling with energy and ideas.

Later in the month, Sonal participated in a similar politically resonant sit-in at Aligarh. In November, she joined a mega street-theatre workshop called Chauraha, with Rati Bartholomew, M.K. Raina, Ram Gopal Bajaj, Dadi Pudumjee, Sadanand Menon, Madan Gopal Singh, G.P. Deshpande, Chandralekha Prabhudas Patel, Tripurari Sharma and a few other writers, performers and political theatre activists. Using theatre's wordiness, this was politics at its most powerful. Along with acts of resistance, Sonal's spectacular performances continued, culminating in the Rajiv Gandhi Excellence Award.

Art and activism cohered again when the group came together on 14 March 1992 for a twelve-hour sit-in at Dadar's Shivaji Park in Bombay. Sonal joined artists, writers, poets and cultural activists, like the Dagar Bandhus, Kishori Amonkar, Ashwini Bhide, Hariprasad Chaurasia, Shivkumar Sharma, Shobha Gurtu, Sultan Khan, Javed Akhtar, Shamim Ahmed, Ravi Shankar, Amol Palekar, Ulhas Kashalkar, Kankana Banerjee, M.F. Hussain, Ali Sardar Jafri, Nida Fazli, Sitara Devi, Dhruv Ghosh, Pandit Jasraj, Dadi Pudumjee, Ghulam Sheikh, Amjad Ali Khan, Shubha Mudgal, C.R. Vyas, Astad Deboo and Raghunath Seth, in a night-long open-air concert.

It was a memorable night, a cultural carnival with a purpose. Hundreds of people hung out with us. Despite our seriousness of purpose, the mood was non-confrontational. We performed against the backdrop of the bold, strong lines of one of Tyeb Mehta's most defining works, *The Falling Figure*, a 10x10 feet canvas, a grim reminder of violent spaces and the demon within.[2]

In April that same year, *Abhinaya Chandrika*, a three-day retrospective of Sonal's dance choreographies, was organized at the Kamani auditorium in Delhi to mark the completion of more than three decades of her performing life. The press speculated about whether her dance life had reached its culmination, its apotheosis.

I let them speculate. And spread out my wings, ready to soar again. I wonder if they heard the frrrrrp sound of my flapping wings.

The year 1992 was significant in many different ways. This was also the year when she finally made the final cut for the Padma awards at a time when she had more or less stopped thinking about them. It was then President R. Venkataraman who called her to the Rashtrapati Bhawan and asked, 'Is it true that the nation hasn't honoured you?' She was awarded the Padma Bhushan that same year. Two years later she was given the Indira Priyadarshini Award for her contribution to dance. The Council of State of Cuba honoured her in 1997 by giving her a medal of friendship when she began a long dance-tour of South and Central America with performances in Havana at the height of the Cuban crisis.

During that tour, in addition to her Bharatanatyam–Odissi repertory, Sonal danced to Pablo Neruda's poetry and had her

Cuban fans weeping tears of exultation. '*Estás Perdido*' ('Where have you been?') was a constant greeting from random people as she walked through Central Havana's Parque Fe del Valle and other streets, charmed by the rundown beauty of a city trapped in time. She listened to stories of cigarette boats that came from Florida to smuggle Cubans to the US and remembered her own efforts to raise money for Cuba. This was in 1992, when the US embargo against the country was at its tightest. India provided Cuba with 10,000 tonnes of wheat and an equal amount of rice in aid. Sonal was asked to ceremonially hand over the consignment to the Cuban ambassador at an event at Mavalankar Hall in Delhi. The aid was piquantly termed 'The Bread of India' by Fidel Castro.

Most artists were wary of a Cuban connection. I admired Fidel Castro and made no bones about it.

Sonal's association with 'Artists against Communalism' ended abruptly when she accepted an invitation to perform at the Global Vision 2000, an event held in August 1993 in Washington to mark the 100th anniversary of Swami Vivekananda's Chicago address at the Parliament of Religions in 1893. One of the many sponsors of the event was the Vishwa Hindu Parishad.[3] Before she returned to India, the jury was out to the drumbeat of demonization.

They stirred up demagoguery against me—the very group of people I had been sharing my political space with. It was an apocalyptic downpour of vitriol. They were not willing to debate with me. They downplayed my involvement with the movement against communalism. I was branded 'right-wing'.

For me, their reaction was a political awakening. I became wary of labels, of identity politics. Wasn't it enough that I was a liberal, a humanist? What gave them the right to be proprietorial about secularism?

She interiorized her sense of disquietude with humour and self-deprecation, focusing on scholarship and research, teaching and performing. Her choreography, *Ektaa*, performed around the same time, was a dance-drama, its central arc being the unity of religions.

I chose to keep away from tired clichés by using the songs and poems of Kabir, Meera, Bulleh Shah[4], the teachings of Guru Nanak and Buddha. My engagement with issues close to my heart continued, not cherry-picked for fashionable polemics, but flowing from my inner convictions.

Plump on success and driven by an overriding need to engage with discourses on social, environmental and gender issues, Sonal began to use her dance space in a radical, new way. Her oeuvre was inviolable, the magic of her creations bewitching an entire generation of dance lovers. Productions like *Atmaayan*, *Mera Bharat*, *Ashta Nayika*, *Samanvaya*, *Mukti*, *Aaj Ki Kanya*, *Panch Kanya*, each more stirring and thought-provoking than the other, were performed. One such production, *Asmita*, a mega-choreography, combined stories and legends connected with each of India's major seven rivers—Saraswati, Ganga, Yamuna, Sindhu, Kaveri,

Godavari and Narmada—woven together in a broad segment called *Sapta-nadi.*

> I established their historical and living identity by depicting one significant incident, legend or myth connected with each in dance and specially composed music. Yamuna, for instance—a river that has much more romantic imagery than any other Indian river simply because she flows through Krishna-land, the *Vraja-bhoomi*, abode of Shri Krishna and Radha. She is the prime witness to the numerous leelas of Krishna, his mischief, his love, his acts of subjugating dark demonic forces so playfully.[5]

If there was one definitive production that marked this time of her life, it was *Draupadi*. Sonal was pushing fifty when she performed *Draupadi* at the Kamani Auditorium in April 1994. The dramatic arc of her choreography, the razor-sharp storytelling, and the staging originality pushed at the limits of what a dance portraiture is capable of. It was an inimitable rendering, stark and tender by turns. She used the fluid movements of Odissi, Bharatanatyam and Chhau to transform herself from one role to the other. That, combined with theatrical abhinaya, set fire to the stage. There was a powerful scorched-earth feel to the production.

> It was a story waiting to be told. At several points in my life, I found myself escaping into Draupadi's life, into her stream of consciousness. She fascinated me all along my childhood, adolescence and youth. Then she began to occupy centre stage in my psyche, and in the five years leading to the production, demanded active attention and delineation. In mainstream

cultural history, Draupadi had been interpreted differently. For me, her story was an intriguing humanist text. Her fiery temperament, her ability to question the injustices heaped on her, her epochal rage and cry for revenge fascinated me, as did her unique friendship with Krishna.[6]

No one could have anticipated the buzz around *Draupadi*. 'Sonal Shines as Draupadi', wrote Ashish Khokar.[7]

First, she is amongst the few soloists who can hold centrestage. Her technique and temperament ensure no dull movements and she renders the role with aplomb. Sonal also depicts what new directions in dance can be all about, even if mixed with theatre. All this talk at seminars serves little purpose unless artists show their worth on stage.[8]

And in the words of noted dance historian and scholar Leela Venkataraman,

Draupadi was a power-packed statement. A seated Draupadi in *muzhumandi*[9] slowly rising to show the emergence from the sacrificial fire was most evocative, accompanied by the chanting. The link with the elements is complete at the end when she is offered the Earth in homage, for she is after all Shakti, Kali and above all Prakriti whose humiliation can only be at the cost of mankind.[10]

Similar words were used by art columnists of newspapers and art journals. She was also feted by scholars and dance critics of the countries where *Draupadi* travelled.

Robin Grove, a scholar from the University of Melbourne, was visibly overwhelmed after her performance at Green Mill Dance Festival. He wrote:

Mansingh, one of India's most celebrated dancers, would be an extraordinary performer anywhere. Her connectedness to the ground, the solidity with which weight is swung between firmly planted feet, her rhetorical largeness of gesture and conscious authority, give her a rare sculptural presence. The richness of detailing suggests the depth of her dance traditions.[11]

Lee Christofis, the dance critic of *The Australian*, added, 'Mansingh's handsome features were strikingly transformed by her subtle mature drama.'[12]

Draupadi dominated the dance performance space for several years. In three years alone following its debut, it was performed at the Nehru Centre in Bombay, at the Kalakshetra in Madras, at Aurobindo Ashram in Auroville, at the Soorya festival in Trivandrum, at the Sangeet Natak Choreography festival in Bangalore, at Quilon in Kerala, on the occasion of a South Asian dialogue in Dhaka, at the Beckett Theatre in the Green Mill Festival in Melbourne in July 1996 and at the Perth International Arts Festival.

By this time Sonal's dance school had settled into a comfortable middle age.

I had a beautiful group of students. I was teaching them to derive beauty and joy from dance. I knew that not every student would develop into a famous danseuse, but

I wanted them to cherish every moment that they spent learning.

Sonal's students were part of her group choreographies and travelled with her wherever the productions took them.

In every new season, Sonal scaled a new level of creativity. She was dramatizing her narrative, creating solo and group choreographies, mixing different dance genres and using an interesting combination of nritta, the non-narrative dance, nritya, the expressional dance, and natya, the dramatic dance. Her choreographies with classical themes continued with productions like *Madhurotsava Devi Durga, Devi Chandrika, Ashta Nayika, Dharma Sringaar, Yugma Geet* and *Vasant Vijay*. Performing at Dharwad, at the old courtyard of the Quila Mubarak in Patiala, in Motihari, Ara and several other small and big towns and cities, she cast a spell in performance after performance, bringing to life forgotten myths and stories through rich imagery and symbolism. She danced to snatches of popular Bollywood songs in a choreography designed for celebration of the tenth anniversary of *Cinemaya*, a film journal. Appropriately titled *Sabarasa*,[13] the songs were interspersed with the swirling notes of different classical ragas when she presented selections from her classical dance repertory. She turned to her solo recitals again and again, every rendition rich, expressive, brimming with life.

Sonal's personal life had grown quiet. She weaned herself away from long-term commitments and made peace with the imperfections of many of her relationships. Some friendships just ebbed away. A section of the press was, however, still obsessing about her 'liaisons'. She continued to be treated to innuendo-laden hostility by fellow artists—and yet, there was room for breeziness and a devil-may-care attitude. Her intellectual energy, beauty and dance continued to cut to the bone of her existence, and her irreverent humour came to her rescue even when something was going awry. She had a bunch of acquaintances of both sexes that she could count as her good friends. There was Ralph Bultjen, a cerebral and quiet academic, part of the Capitol Hill think tank, who visited every year bringing her beautiful baskets of flowers, Ajit Sud and his wife Loveleen, Sudarshan Agarwal, Nandini Ramani, Veena Shroff, Anand Kumar, Jasleen Dhamija, Salman Haider and Shridev Sharma—a lively entourage of friends who became her surrogate family.

The year 1995 was drenched in sorrow. It began with the death of one of her closest friends, Madhu Limaye, on 8 January. In his death, the country lost a celebrated civil liberty activist, scholar, leader and parliamentarian.

I lost someone I had leaned on all these years. The process of reconnecting with life after his death was difficult.

In July, she lost her father after spending six blissful weeks with him a few days before his death, one of the longest spells in recent memory. His death left her emotionally incontinent. She turned to her mother, rebonding with her in ways she had not thought possible earlier.

The next major blow came on 2 September 1998 when she lost Jiwan Pani. Jiwan Pani lived a life that was larger than life. A poet, scholar and aesthete, he inspired many artists, theatre persons and dancers in his lifetime. An accomplished person who unfortunately became a victim of vicious politics at the Sangeet Natak Akademi, he was not spared even when he retired. His personal files 'disappeared' from the administrative wing. His pension was wrongly withheld. He was made to go back to Orissa and dig out past records. He did that, but the Akademi's staff once again misplaced the records.

> They broke his spirit. He had to borrow money from a friend to fight a legal battle in the high court. All this took a toll. He had a sudden, massive cardiac arrest. Later, when I took over as the chairperson of the Akademi, I asked the administration to produce the 'lost' documents in two hours, threatening to dismiss them if they failed. The documents naturally surfaced immediately. When I delivered the cheque to his wife, she broke down and said, 'No one but you remembers him.' I told her that I would always stand by her.

Sonal honoured her mentor by starting the Jiwan Pani Memorial Festival, a yearly event held on two successive days at the Stein Auditorium of the India Habitat Centre in Delhi. The first festival, inaugurated by the President of India on 30 November 1998 featured Kathak by Pandit Birju Maharaj, Bharatanatyam by Poorva Dutt and Odissi by Sonal and Rashmi Ranjan Jena. The festival brings different art forms together. Hence, if in the tenth chapter of the festival, the performance of the day was Lushin Dubey's play, *Bitter Chocolate*, a solo piece on child abuse directed by Arvind Gaur, the eleventh chapter had Kathakali by Kalamandalam Gopi, Kathak by Aditi Mangaldas, Vilasini

Natyam by Swapna Sundari and an Odissi and Bharatanatyam jugalbandi by Sonal's students, Pallavi Pramanik and Pallavi Saran Gujral.

Sonal's dance continued to travel with her to different countries—thirty-eight countries in the 1990s alone, and about the same in the first decade of the 2000s. What was significant was that she was working the seminar and lecture circuit in universities, art museums and think tanks. Her long dance tours to North America and Canada in 2000 and then again in 2001 were dotted with seminars and lectures. She delivered lectures at the Museum of Civilization located across the Ottawa river in Gatineau, at the McGill University in Montreal, at the Emory College in Atlanta, at the Davidson College in North Carolina, following it up with lec-dems on the invitation of SPICMACAY at the Rudder Theatre in A&M University at Texas in 2003. Reporting for the *Gazette* after Sonal's lecture at McGill, columnist and feature writer Donna Nebenzahl wrote:

Sonal Mansingh's hands tell a thousand tales. Her eyes convey a host of emotions. The acclaimed Indian dancer calls her work social transformation through dance 'for those who are silenced or don't have a voice'. Today violence is claiming us, she told an audience at a recent appearance in Montreal. 'We need the arts to create beauty in our lives. Art and dance are our last refuge.'[14]

One of the highpoints of this period was Sonal's participation in the World Dance Conference 2000 in Tokyo held in celebration of the new millennium. She teamed up with the great Noh[15] master, Hideo Kanze, for a lec-dem on the salient features of Odissi and Noh.

This was truly a challenge. Noh represents an extremely codified classical tradition. I was lecturing and performing with Hideo Kanze, the living national treasure of Japan. When our session got over, we were complimented by everyone present there and told that we had created history.

In April 2001, Sonal performed on the occasion of the International Dance Day[16] at Maison de I'UNESCO in Paris, followed by a performance at the prestigious World Dance Alliance Asia-Pacific Dance Bridge[17] in Singapore, organized as a Singapore Arts Festival in-conjunction event. An Indian Council for Cultural Relations (ICCR)-sponsored tour to Sri Lanka was next on her itinerary. This tour has a special place in Sonal's collage of memories. Her deliciously driven performance got her a special letter of appreciation from a woman she admires deeply, Chandrika Kumaratunga, the fifth President of Sri Lanka:

My dear Sonal, I am writing to express my sincere appreciation of the magnificent performance of Bharata Natyam by you, the other evening. Thank you very much for a beautiful evening. The dancing was simply exquisite. My children and I were enamoured by the recital. At least for a short while, I was able to move away from the trouble and turmoil of the human world to a more exalted heavenly plane of blissful serenity. It is such memories that I treasure in life.

Sonal's dance tour to Kenya, Uganda, Algeria, Sudan and Egypt in 2006 was another unique experience, much of its appeal lying in the heady excitement of performing within volatile political borders, different cultural sensitivities and ethnic diversity. In Khartoum, where the two Niles converge, she performed at the National Theatre to a predominantly male audience. There were blinking fairy lights strung across the theatre, but it was Sonal's glowing presence and the beauty of her performance that lit up the stage and had the audience catching their breath. Sudan at that point had just seen a peace accord that ended decades of violent conflict between the north and the south. Sonal wanted to do her bit in healing the bruised country. She thought nothing of bumping along potholed roads on blisteringly hot days for open-air performances in places as distant as 600 kilometres from Khartoum, or weathering the awful condition of her dysfunctional hotel that was bereft of running water.

Thundering applauses and standing ovations followed her as Sonal crossed borders and performed in different countries. She also found time to drive through red-dirt roads of the Maasai Plains, crossing lines of army ants and slender-tailed mongooses, through clumps of Africa's wooden elephants, the baobab trees, to camp in a grove of fig, ebony and wild olive trees in a national park near Nairobi. Her solo Bharatanatyam performances included elements of visual poetry created by her in the form of nature navarasa, much to the aesthetic delight of her smitten audiences.

In India too, Sonal's time was crammed with performances, talks and seminars. She was nominated as one of the trustees of the Indira Gandhi National Centre for Arts. Time now seemed shorter, more urgent, but she managed occasional breaks in her routine for one-off events like sashaying down the runway for a fashion extravaganza organized by a friend, flagging off an eco-friendly initiative by planting a bamboo sapling at the Raj Bhawan in Chennai, presenting the *Hindustan Times*'s most stylish award to Nidhi Razdan,[18] or taking to the ramp at the Wills Lifestyle India Fashion Week.

There were serious commitments waiting to be addressed. One of them related to a project that had a life-changing potential and had obsessed her for a long, long time—teaching dance to prisoners of the Tihar Jail in Delhi. She managed to see her dream through in 1998.

It was an amazing experience. When I was asked to choose, I chose Jail 1 that housed the most dangerous convicts. I had to break many barriers to reach out to them but I persevered, powered by the belief that art purges the soul. By the end of my workshop, they developed a genuine love for classical dance. The result was a special choreography for the International Day of Human Rights with nine lifers along with members of my troupe. We decided to call our production *Manavata*,[19] and staged it on 10 December 1998 at the Siri Fort auditorium in Delhi in the presence of the prime minister, home minister and several other dignitaries. It was a transformational process for the life convicts. They told me that I had ignited something within them that they didn't know existed.

Sonal poured her knowledge of Indian classical dances into a book on the classical dance traditions of India, called *Classical Dances*.[20] A part of the Incredible India series, the book provides a kaleidoscopic description of different facets of Bharatanatyam, Odissi, Kathak, Kathakali, Mohiniattam, Manipuri, Kuchipudi and Sattriya.[21] In its scholarly effort to keep India's collective dance history alive, the book bridges the space between different epochs, seeing change essentially as part of a nuanced historical continuum. The photographs used in this book are from the photo archive of Avinash Pasricha, a well-known dance photographer.

Sonal received the Padma Vibhushan, India's second highest civilian award, in 2003, making her the second woman dancer in India to receive this award after Balasaraswati.

It was unbelievable. I was rehearsing with a student from Seattle when a TV news reporter came with the startling news. I was dizzy with excitement when I heard about it.

Receiving the award on 3 April from the then President Dr A.P.J. Abdul Kalam, Sonal said that it was special honour and proud moment for Indian classical dance.

The next major milestone was Sonal's appointment as chairperson of the Sangeet Natak Akademi on 19 December 2003 by the NDA government in power[22] at that time. Functioning as the apex body of performing arts in the country, the Akademi nurtured music, dance, puppetry and theatre of every genre—tribal, folk, martial, classical. Overdosed on fame, Sonal dreamt of taking the work of her predecessors forward by creating a beautiful space that would enliven existing traditions, and resuscitate endangered, comatose art forms. She opened up the Akademi for discussions and deliberations on what needed to be done, testing and pushing existing boundaries, creating new ones.

Gripped by excitement, she reclaimed land for the Kathak Kendra and tried to tone up the administration. Incompetence and a complete disregard for rules at the Akademi had reached a tipping point. It was a difficult situation, but Sonal decided to hug it out.

On 29 April 2004, International Dance Day, we sought an appointment with the President, and then about thirty-two of us went to Rashtrapati Bhawan for tea and some intense brainstorming. In the evening, the lawns were all lit up. We invited Birju Maharaj as the chief guest. Twenty-six groups representing different styles performed to more than 2,000 art lovers. There was comradeship and joy.

The joy was chimeric. On 22 May 2004, a coalition of the Congress-led United Progressive Alliance (UPA), with external support from Left political parties, formed the new government at the Centre. Sonal was caught between allegations and counter-allegations, conflicting political agendas and serious sexist assumptions. The rumour mill was relentless, in a full kitchen-sink mode, throwing in wild revelations, red herrings and scandals. She saw many of her initiatives being sand-papered and eroded. All her excitement greiged out.

By the middle of 2005, Sonal found herself in the spotlight for the wrong reasons. A few well-known artists resigned from the Akademi's general council and executive board[23] in protest against what they called her 'autocratic style'.

It was all very well designed and orchestrated. No fierce polemics, no dialogue. I learnt of the en masse resignations from newspapers. The charges were frivolous. One of them was that I wanted to change the name of the Akademi. A significant fact in this context is that when the Akademi was set up in 1952, it was mistakenly named 'Sangeet Natak' leaving out the dance component. No one bothered to rectify this anomaly. When I took over, I suggested the name Natya, a word that includes music, dance and drama— taking inspiration from Bharata's *Natyashastra*, a detailed compendium on the performing arts. This, however, was still under discussion. Another charge was that I had ordered audio recordings of proceedings of the council board and committee meetings. This was truly ironic. The decision to record was the result of the clamour raised by executive board members about their ideas being 'misrepresented' in the minutes of the board meeting. Fundamentally, the issue was that I had disturbed a well-entrenched nexus that was running the Akademi as its fiefdom.

There were vicious personal attacks, the worst of which were related to my mother's nomination for the Padma awards in 2004. The insinuation was that I had used my proximity to BJP leaders to get the state government in Gujarat to nominate her. My mother's work with the Dangs tribals is too well known to be debated, and the fact is that my ninety-two-year-old mother received her award after the President visited the Dangs and saw her work. They also insinuated that my own selection to the post of chairperson was due to my proximity to the then prime minister. They attacked the contents of a CD-ROM produced during my tenure. They sought and won the support of Left leaders like Harkishan Singh Surjeet in their campaign against me.

There were counter-protests too when Sonal went to present her case about the allegations levelled against her to the then culture minister, S. Jaipal Reddy. Three of the executive board members—Swapna Sundari, Kumudini Lakhia and Nandini Ramani—accompanied her. Twenty-three leading artists wrote a letter to the culture minister saying they were extremely unhappy with the vilification campaign against her. Girish Karnad, who was chairperson of the Akademi from 1988 to 1993, wrote to the President of India praising Sonal as 'one of the great artists of our time'. He noted,

> Once a person is appointed to this post, she or he should be removable only if proven guilty of criminal misdemeanour. If she or he were to be removed on the basis of emotive criticism or mere difference of opinion on matters of policy or on grounds of political affiliation, it will bring the Akademi to a grinding halt.[24]

None of this helped.

Trapped in what was quickly turning out to be a Kafkaesque nightmare, Sonal was replaced by Congressman Ram Niwas Mirdha in June 2005 by a presidential order.

> Let me clarify that I was replaced by a new appointee as pointed out in the official letter from the ministry of culture, which said that the President of India was pleased to appoint Mirdha in my place. The then President, Dr A.P.J. Abdul Kalam, in fact called me to see him at the Rashtrapati Bhawan on 22 May and showed me the draft of the letter. The draft used the word 'removed'. He struck

that out, substituting it with 'replaced'. He was also most apologetic about what had happened.

She took another hard knock when her Bharatanatyam guru and mentor Ubhayakar Shivaram Krishna Rao died on 6 March the same year.

Sonal counts her trip to Kailash Mansarovar as the most intense, redemptive experience of her life at this point.

Shiva as Nataraj is the Lord of Dance. Not for nothing has Carl Sagan drawn an analogy between the cosmic dance of Nataraj and the study of the cosmic dance of subatomic particles. A bronze statue of the dancing Nataraj in an aureole of flames, lifting his left leg and balancing over a demon who symbolizes ignorance, has been installed at the CERN (European Organization for Nuclear Research) complex in Geneva. To dance at Kailash, Shiva's abode, precious to one-fifth of humankind, was my dream.

In July 2006, Sonal joined a group led by Swami Chidanand Saraswati[25] to participate at the Saga Dawa[26] festival at Kailash. It was a multi-day trek, through high altitudes and unpredictable mountain weather, braving extreme tiredness and altitude sickness. This, however, did not result in Sonal taking a less rose-tinted view of the journey. The group went via Nepal through rocky, hostile terrain to reach the immigration post of the border town of Zangmu. Their luggage was held back for a couple of days by the hostile immigration officers. It was pouring. Wet to the skin, Sonal's group camped on the banks of Lake Pigutso. Many of her fellow travellers returned, but she was a ball of infectious energy, and continued the trek with what remained of her group and hundreds of Tibetan pilgrims in their ankle-length dresses and twirling prayer wheels.

The long trek stopped only when they reached the blue expanse of the Mansarovar Lake and saw Mount Kailash.

When I saw the ice-covered dome of Kailash, gleaming like a diamond against the clear blue sky, I fell to the ground and wept. It was a presence beyond words. I could almost see my beloved Nataraj sitting there in eternal meditation.

After finishing their *kosh parikrama* or circumambulation, the group camped by the side of the lake, its waterline awash with gulls, sandpipers and hundreds of other birds.

I dipped in the deep blue water and could feel it purify not only my body but also my soul.

Overwhelmed, ecstatic, Sonal prayed first to Devi, the female cosmic energy force driving Shiva, and then performed the Bhagawati *stuti* in Odissi on the Ashtapath plateau at the height of 16,000 feet. It was an experience like no other. It also made her the only dancer to dance before the sacred mountain on the roof of the world.[27]

Awards and honours kept coming Sonal's way. She received the Kalidas Samman[28] in 2006. She was honoured with the title 'Kameshwari' by the Adi Shaktipeeth of Kamakhya[29] in Assam. She was conferred three honorary doctorates—from the G.B. Pant University, Sambalpur University and KIIT University, Bhubaneswar. She was also appointed as honorary professor at the University of Delhi. A documentary made by celebrated film-maker Prakash Jha to assess her legacy won the National Film Award for the best non-feature film in 2002. A biography in Hindi, *Devapriya*,[30] written by poet and author Yatindra Mishra followed.

* * *

It's a warm, autumnal morning, on 5 October 2015, Sonal's mother's 102nd birthday. We are at the Ritambhara Vishwa Vidyapeeth, a residential school for poor, tribal girls established by her mother in 1974. The school nestles in the hills of the Dangs, a district in Gujarat. I am here at a time when she is clearly very sick. The celebrations are low-key. It is a period of intense anxiety. Sonal, on the brink of exhaustion, keeps me insulated from the dark storms brewing within her as we resume our conversations.

Did you gain a bit of Machiavellian wisdom after your Sangeet Natak Akademi experience? Any life lessons? Or did it just become a part of your turbulent narrative of belief and betrayal?

No, I just hugged the entire experience out. It is like it never happened. It gave me a greater impetus to perform and create.

Would it be right to say that in some ways your life has been like Draupadi's?

Draupadi is a mirror in which every woman faces herself. She has been my inspiration. Like her, I have never let any evidence of misogyny go unchallenged in my life.

175

Irawati Karve in her classic *Yuganta* is dismissive of the idea that Draupadi was a proto-feminist. She saw her as being a cog in the wheel of a strongly patriarchal order.

There have been many engagements with the text. Every engagement comes with certain domain assumption. For me, she is Panchali, a woman with great intellect who has studied logic mathematics. Born from *agnigarbha*, a womb of fire, she is Prakriti, the powerful cosmic principle of creation and dissolution. She is Kali, the fascinating, dark goddess who plays with time, creating it and devouring it. Her demand for revenge is in the form of blood. When she is pulled by her long, curly, flame-like hair by Dussasana, she leaves her entangled hair open until washed by the blood of Dussasana.

The Kauravas have been taking heat for their acts of misogyny, but Draupadi also holds a mirror to the chauvinism of the Pandava brothers, especially Yudhishthira, a flawed, weak-kneed, spineless man.

The story of Draupadi's humiliation reaches beyond narrative time. We have not internalized what Vyas was trying to communicate. Violence against women and sexualization of that violence continues. That violence eventually destroyed Hastinapur. It is destroying the fabric of our society. At another level, by denuding earth–nature–*prakriti*, we are inviting holocausts of unimaginable proportions.

How important have feminist movements been in your life?

Feminist movements have been on my radar. I did support the politics of inclusion that shaped feminist discourse in the 1960s. But by the late 1970s I could see the movement splintering, and opted to keep myself away from the maelstrom of competing politics. Someone rightly said that feminism should be like a massive patchwork quilt capable of amalgamating individual ideas and strengths. Dance helps me dress up my feminism in innovative ways. It helps me raise a voice against the most egregious form of sexism and patriarchy.

What do you think of Femen, the feminist group known for their topless, rather burlesque protests or SlutWalks?

Don't they in some ways reinforce objectification of the female body? I like to keep away from all forms of extremism, even sextremism.

Was your decision to collaborate with leading theatre directors, musicians and visual artists of the day for *Draupadi* inspired by Martha Graham?

I did team up with theatre director Amal Allana. Later, Ratan Thiyam helped out with lighting and the use of the flute in our soundtrack. I used a good light designer who understood the poetics of light. For my first performance, stage designer Nissar Allana created a revolutionary set design by juxtaposing interesting theatre props with nude male mannequins representing male aggression.

I used sartorial advice from friends while putting together the costumes, using my own sense of aesthetics to wear colours that portrayed the essential Draupadi. But nothing like what Martha Graham did. Our scales were completely different.

Martha Graham used fashion designers like Donna Karan and Calvin Klein, composers like William Schuman and Gian Carlo Menotti, and stage props by leading sculptor Isamu Noguchi to transform her dance.

You have always been somewhat self-deprecating about your body of work. In an interview in 1991 you said that what you were doing was not terribly innovative. Looking back at productions like *Draupadi*, do you still feel that you broke no new ground?

Tradition is always alive, in a constant state of motion and change. What I have done is to use metaphors sleeping in our classical texts to create choreographies that are reflective of the complex interplay between the past and present. I was called the high priestess of innovation even when I was in my twenties and thirties. But my most important ideas are evolving now. I am in a process of constant change, constant reinvention. For me dance is a sensual, passionate act driven by my mind. I am rewriting the rules of performing.

How much has technology impacted classical dance?

A good deal. Technology has transformed dance. Look at lighting—its use is far more textured than it was earlier. The fact that it can dramatize stage has finally been recognized. Lighting designers are no longer faceless, and the same can be said for stage and sound designers. However, my instincts are still low-tech. I engage with high technology fairly sparingly and feel that it leads to the erosion of imagination.

Your choreographies have engaged with politics at different levels, especially sexual politics. What have been the dominant global trends?

One of the greatest dancers of the early twentieth century, Isadora Duncan, was a Bolshevik. She choreographed a radical dance piece, *Internationale*, and staged it at Bolshoi in the presence of Lenin. Martha Graham's *Deep Song* was a political commentary on the Spanish Civil War. There was something deeply political about the dance–theatre created by Pina Bausch. There are young choreographers engaging with the wars in Syria and Iraq. In UK, a group called X6 has been revolutionizing dance spaces. Moving Being, another group, incorporates feminist texts from Germaine Greer in their choreographies. The list is endless.

I read somewhere that you found Pina Bausch's work too angsty. Your own favourite rasa is sringara.

American critic Ariane Croce accused Bausch of using the pornography of pain. Her dance was evocative of human frailty and brutality, sexual violence. But in hindsight, I can't deny that she transformed the possibilities of modern dance. The small town of Wuppertal where she lived and taught became a Mecca for dance. For me, yes, aesthetic pleasure or rasa which invokes a feeling of delight or ananda is important for any work of art. A great work of art disturbs, moves, incites, but culminates in aesthetic relish.

12

A New World Coming into View

Around the fiftieth year of her dance life, Sonal added the *Naatya Katha* to her oeuvre. Inspired by an ancient form[1] of storytelling, her naatya kathas crackle with intellectual energy and emotional warmth. With her image-drenched narration and abhinaya, poetic tone and charmingly nuanced singing, the kathas are an incredible visual and spiritual experience. Her first naatya katha, *Krishna Ranga Raachee*,[2] was performed in Delhi in August 2009. Organized by Ajit Sood[3] in the ballroom of Le Méridien hotel in Delhi, Sonal's katha enthralled the select audience from the time it began in Brajbhoomi with news of the birth of a beautiful boy to Yashoda and Nanda. A slew of lovely flowers accessorized the photo-ready ballroom. The backdrop had bushels of roses, strings of jasmine, vines of greenery. It was like performing in Vrindavan.[4]

Sonal performed with abandon for three long hours, using portions of the Bhagavata Purana[5] and Bhagavad Gita, poems of the *ashta chhaap* poets,[6] Meera, Surdas and Jayadeva, Gujarati compositions by Narsinh Mehta and the lyrics of Sitakant Mahapatra to recreate the blue god's life, her consummate performance winning over the most hardened sceptics.

Sonal has performed different versions of the *Krishna Katha* many times, in contexts as varied as the Swami Haridas Mahotsav in Vrindavan, before a small audience at Ravi Shankar's residence in San Diego, California, at the Ravi Shankar Centre in Delhi on the occasion of Ravi Shankar's ninety-sixth birth anniversary, on George Harrison's seventy-third birth anniversary on 6 February 2016, at different sabhas in Chennai, at the Hutheesing Haveli, just outside the gates of the old walled city of Ahmedabad, at the Birla Sabhaghar in Jaipur, at the 'Remembering Rukmini Devi' Festival at Kalakshetra in March 2016, at Guwahati at the Srimanta Sankardev Kalakshetra on 25 October 2016 and at the Raj Bhawan at Bhubaneswar—altogether, in more than twenty cities in India and abroad.

> Every katha has a unique narrative momentum and gives me space to lead it where it interests me most.

Sonal has an intimate, creative relationship with her audience that drives her to interpret her naatya kathas in different ways. The narratives are not set in stone. Every katha seems to undergo a magical makeover, unshackling itself from its past rendition. She uses an ambience-specific mix of languages like Sanskrit, Hindi, English, Gujarati and Oriya in different contexts to match the mood of the audience.[7] She engages, she provokes, she plays amazing mind games, even while keeping everything, including the backdrop, very simple.

The evening unfolds with minimal stage settings. Just a central seat for me, with the musicians seated on two sides and a screen for the back-projection of miniatures and paintings depicting highlights from selected episodes for the evening's presentation. I have been wearing saris for my kathas, not a costume as with dance. I am the *kathakaar*, the narrator, singer and interpreter. There should be no distraction from Krishna. There is no bravado, no ego, only a heart full of passion and eagerness to share the joy and delight in being with Krishna for an uninterrupted length of time. My consciousness is already heightened to a pitch when I can no longer wait. With the formalities over, I enter the darkened stage with only a stream of amber light illuminating the musicians already standing in their white Indian attire with *angavastram*s.[8]

Many of Sonal's dance choreographies have reincarnated as naatya kathas. *Draupadi* and *Panch Kanya* that have addressed the loaded issue of sexual politics. Extraordinary stories of women in her naatya katha—*Stree* presented on International Women's Day on 8 March 2016. Stories that have a thematic resonance and that raise contemporary issues. And then there are river stories pointing to ecocide. The story of Krishna's subjugation of Kaaliya the cobra king responsible for poisoning the river Yamuna with bilious yellow-green fumes. The dramatic story of Krishna dancing on Kaaliya's head.[9] This interpretation has given rise to *Eco-puran*, a performance designed for children and staged in schools and pop-up events.

*Devi Katha*s performed in tomatoey red sarees are important because without Devi or Shakti, even Shiva would be *shava*,[10] incapable of stirring. Using legends, myths and a plethora of literary texts, she creates an interpretation that feels contemporary, capable of fixing the most sordid existential angst. The philosophical underpinnings of Hans Georg Godamer's[11] hermeneutic cycle are clearly at work in her naatya kathas. It is not she who seems to address the texts of tradition but it is the canonical texts that seem to drive her performances.

One of Sonal's favourite kathas is based on ashtapadis from the *Geet Govind*. Jayadeva's poem has fired the imagination of generations of musicians and dancers. Her own passion for *Geet Govind* is nothing if not ardent. In her compositions, Sonal opens up a beautiful world of metaphors through which this deceptively simple, timeless and universal play of passion between Radha and Krishna unfolds.

I get my fix of ananda showering the stage with sringara rasa to play out the relationship between Radha and Krishna. A playful abandon sharpens my storytelling. I create a joyful mood while playing out the sensual, erotic, love-related themes.

Sonal slips into different personas with ease. She is Radha, the source of life and love. She is Krishna. She is the *sakhi* (friend). Even the tangible and the intangible forms of nature seem to take a definitive form in her performances.

A trained vocalist, Sonal sings portions of the lyrics used in the narrative, while Bankim Sethi sings the rest. She intersperses her singing, dancing and narration with little speeches.

The *Abhinayadarpan* written by Nandikeshvara,[12] one of the greatest theories on the stagecraft of ancient India, includes a verse on the ten qualities of a classical dance performer. One of the qualities mentioned is *vacho* or speech. So what I am doing has in a sense been ordained by the canonical texts. I sing, I act, I dance, I narrate, I address the audience. I share with them the totality of what I have—my body, soul, expressions, moods, feelings, experiences, ideas, thoughts. I am very happy doing this.

The glamour and charm of being on the small screen as an incarnation of *guru shreshtha*, the supreme teacher, was realized when she conceptualized a dance reality show for Doordarshan, called *Bharat ki Shaan—Rum Jhum*. Flagged off in October 2013, the show was planned as a competition between Indian classical dance forms and non-Indian dance forms,[13] and created much more than a bubble-gum buzz. Sonal was in the hot seat two days a week, diva-like in exquisite sarees, week after week for fifty-six episodes, judging the contestants.

The show was paced like a soap opera. We sometimes had to shoot two episodes in one go. The dancers who were judged on their technical, expressive and creative abilities complained of not having enough rehearsal time. I too felt spaced out, but we endured. And if Indian classical dances brought in gravitas, then a peppy cha-cha, a raunchy rumba and dancers trying to moonwalk or imitate Kevin Bacon's hop-kicks also brought joy to the dance floor.

Everyone on the sets took their cues from Sonal. Her own perspective and dance-related vignettes were delivered as

Guru Gyaan.[14] She was inundated with blog posts, tweets and emails from a growing, young fan-base. The programme managed to broaden interest in classical and non-classical dance forms, gave her diehard fans a sense of déjà vu, opened the door for young dancers and catapulted many of them to stardom. Two male dancers from the show, Kathak performer Quincy Charles and Sattriya performer Dipjyoti Singh, were invited to perform at the twelfth Jiwan Pani Memorial Festival. Kathak dancers Kadam and Raina Parikh were invited to perform on the occasion of International Women's Day in 2016 at the Stein auditorium by the Centre for Indian Classical Dances.

Sonal remains justifiably proud of her body of work as a performer, teacher and dance theorist. Not really ready to trust anyone, she choreographs her compositions to the minutest details. Her itinerary continues to be back-breaking with a minimum of three to four outstation performances a month. In December 2015, she had six back-to-back performances in Chennai, dancing for the Narad Gana Sabha, the Brahma Gana Sabha, Shri Krishna Gana Sabha, and the Art Festival 2015, Bharatiya Vidya Bhawan's Natya Utsav. She rang in the new year by dancing Bharatanatyam at the Ethiraja Kalyana Nilayam at Alwarpet. Performing naatya kathas at programmes organized by the Sangeet Natak Akademi, North-East Centre at Agartala, Imphal, Guwahati, Tezpur and Dibrugarh in October 2016. And this is how it goes on. Performances, lectures, panel discussions, opening speaker at a seminar on reproductive biology and sexuality in AIIMS, visiting professor at the Banaras Hindu University . . . She is truly unstoppable, with a kick-ass attitude at work.

The hot ticket in contemporary choreographies is Sonal's operatic production, *When the Gods Meet*, based on Indo-Greek mythological libretto. The production, which debuted at the G.D. Birla Sabhaghar stage in Kolkata on 14 November 2013, was as much about music as it was about dance. The music was composed by sitar maestro, Shubhendra Rao, his wife, renowned cellist Saskia Rao-de Haas, and their team of musicians, French–American composer, concert pianist and organ player, Ariane Gray Hubert, Bankim Sethi and Sonal herself—bringing different musical genres together.

A tapestry of nine emotions, the navarasa, was woven by using Indian myths performed by her group of dancers while she played the role of the storyteller or *sutradhaar*, who knits different narratives together.[15] She appeared as Sumati, the chief queen-consort of Kaaliya, the king of cobras, and Lakshmi, the wife of Vishnu. For the Greek myth of Eros, the god of love, and Psyche, the woman he falls in love with, she took on the role of Psyche's jealous sister. She was the friend of Europa, the lovely human princess courted by Zeus, the king of gods. The Greek myths in Latin American and Western dance forms were performed by Sandip Soparrkar[16] and his group.

The compelling choreography ended with the marriage of Shiva and Parvati, the cosmic pair in Indian mythology, and the marriage of Greek earth goddess Gaia with Uranus, the sky god, danced vibrantly against a textured lighting dramatizing the stage. The production enthralled music and dance aficionados and was given a standing ovation.[17] Sonal repeated the production at the Kamani auditorium a month later, using children from the AHLCON International School[18] to unravel the Greek myths in an exquisitely calibrated performance that fizzed with charm. Since then, *When the Gods Meet* has travelled to many different venues.

Sonal is one among the nine jewels, or *navratna*,[19] chosen by Prime Minister Narendra Modi for the Swachh Bharat Abhiyaan or the Clean India Campaign. She has taken the campaign forward by using the performing arts space to promote the importance of keeping the mind, body and environment clean. Themed *Abhilasha* or aspiration, the twelfth chapter of the Jiwan Pani Festival in 2015 featured evocative music and dance from student groups, their classical training embellishing their Swachh-related repertory. On 12 December 2015, in an event organized by the Ministry of Urban Development, Government of India, she used Odissi, Bharatanatyam, Manipuri and Mohiniattam dance forms in an open-air performance at New Delhi's India Gate to spread awareness—another instance of the medium itself becoming the message. She has plans to use open spaces in public parks and heritage sites for her dance- and music-based campaign, allowing herself a cautious optimism that change will eventually occur.

Her choreographies still on overdrive, Sonal shows absolutely no signs of slowing down and is clearly enjoying this time of her life. She has set herself free, unencumbered and carefree in a way that's not studied, unfettered by the burdens of memory and regret, choosing to celebrate her mother's life when she passed away after living an incredible life on 25 April 2016.

Are people around her star-struck? Yes, they are. She is a legend. She has received the country's highest accolades and has been a rage internationally. Hers has been the life most others can only dream of. Her stardom might make one feel apprehensive of a cultish environment around her, but up close she is delightfully unstarry and childlike. She loves silly funny gags and has the ability to transform the most ordinary anecdote into an unforgettable, irreverent parable. Unflinchingly strong, with needle-sharp clarity on most issues, she tires of outworn, outlived ideas easily. She is disturbed when her suggestions on cultural renaissance do not gain the traction they should, or when she sees dance being indifferently treated in a school curriculum, and acts up a storm when she is upset.

* * *

It is the evening of 5 November 2016 at Purana Qila, one of the oldest forts in Delhi. Bewitching in a black skirt, a short black blouse and an orange dupatta, Sonal stands with her troupe to take the final curtain call after her performance of a new naatya katha, Krishna Leela Madhuri, *a little overwhelmed with the deluge of love and admiration.*

Your kathas are such an interesting frieze in your body of work. What led you to them? Did they start like Isadora Duncan's celebrated barefoot dances that began one intoxicated night when she could not perform in her whisky-soused shoes?

No such luck. It was quite a sedate beginning. A bunch of us were partying together on Krishnashtami[20] when I was asked to sing. I sang, explained the meaning of the verses, used abhinaya to nuance the meaning and voila, naatya katha was born.

The kathas seem to play mind games, never letting the audience off the hook.

Naatya kathas are rooted in our tradition of oral narratives. They allow me the flexibility of taking my audience into the interior of a thought, an idea, a concept. They give me a chance to get my teeth into contemporary social, environmental and gender discourses in a visceral manner. The timelessness and universality of themes connects them to both the young and the old.

Though not yoked together, *Draupadi*, *Panch Kanya* and *Aaj Ki Kanya* make for a provocative trilogy.

Yes, *Panch Kanya* is in the form of mini-narratives centred on the lives of Ahalya, Draupadi, Kunti, Tara and Mandodari, women living in dystopian worlds ruled by patriarchy, raising the question: 'Has anything changed?' *Aaj Ki Kanya* explores the dawning of a new consciousness and is assertive of women's right to equality.

How important is a dancer's body?

Extremely. A dancer's body belongs to a public space, objectified, open to voyeurism. One wouldn't like the audience to comment on wobbling flesh. An Indian classical dancer needs a toned and supple body, but beyond a degree one does not need to obsess over its shape and size. Remember Balasaraswati. She was comely, a little plump by contemporary standards. But her body had gravitas, a sensuality that remains unmatched. It is in the context of Western ballets that dancers need to conform to the ideal of androgynous bodies draped in body-hugging tunics and leotards.

Have you ever gone through a period of body anxiety?

Yes, but only for a short period. My mother had taught me not to obsess about my looks. That mantra worked. So clearly, no prima donna bullshit for me. Even now I am perfectly happy in my skin. I have never needed a tummy tuck (*laughs*).

Your skin is completely unlined. How have you stopped it from ageing?

Believe me, it's not Botox or things like vampire facials! I could never consider using anything aggressive to ease time's predations. I must give credit to my genes, my jar of Pond's cold cream (*laughs*) and dance that permeates my body with joy and love, my manic pulse rate when I create something new.

You seem to have found time for far more than would fit into a life. Have you ever felt the need to downsize?

Not really. I think dance pushes up my metabolism. I take classes. Go through my administrative work. Write. Compose. Travel. Perform. Brainstorm ideas. My time passes in a blur of deadlines. But I also manage some downtime with my friends—long walks in Lodhi Garden, theatre, concerts, a movie with a large packet of popcorn, motorbike rides when I am in Auroville with my friend, Arjun, haute cuisine in my favourite restaurants, cordon bleu moments in my own kitchen.

Don't you conduct autopsies?

Compellingly, when a project fails or when a friendship ends.

Money?

It's quite gauche to talk about it, but don't we all need it?

Is there a cultural space for classical dances?

Yes and no. Sometimes I feel that there is a herd of elephants occupying that space.

Is the classical dance audience ageing?

Yes, there are ageing regulars, but many young people too. Expats who converge to explore the Indian dance heritage, young students. There are intense moments in performances, epiphanic moments, when the audience collectively holds its breath—then all the differences melt.

You have a book-lined home. What are your favourites amongst them?

K.M. Munshi's *Krishnavatara* volumes in Gujarati, Anais Nin's journals, Han Suyin's *A Many-Splendoured Thing*,

Ramesh Menon's *Blue God*, David Niven's *The Moon's a Balloon*, C. Rajagopalachari's *Mahabharata*, Vikram Seth's *The Golden Gate*.

A book that obsessed you?

It would have to be Jayadeva's *Geet Govind*.

Any specific political ideologies at this point of time?

There is a general perception that I tend to align with right-wing political groups. It used to bother me, but doesn't any more. What matters to me is my own personal manifesto rooted in the beauty of classical cultural traditions, literature, music and dance.

In your critique of the Left, sometimes the aggression seems unwarranted.

It is validated by personal experience. I dislike the tendency on their part to see the world in stark binary terms. How brain-dead is that!

How much longer do you expect to dance?

I know that everything is finite; my dance life too is finite. But right now dance is the focal point of my life, the reason for my being. What keeps me going is the constant obsession to create, and to share the beauty that I have experienced. It's a long journey. I may have to take many more births as a dancer.

Have you ever wanted to exile yourself from your legacy?

No, that's me. That's all I have.

If someone was to do your biographical portrait, who would play you?

If I had a choice and if Marlene Dietrich would have been alive, it would have been her.

Acknowledgements

This book draws its life and energy from Sonal Mansingh. I owe her a great deal, and sometimes worry about questions that remained unasked, thoughts that could have been further probed.

I owe a great deal to my father too—to the smile that lit up my life and his scholarly analysis of cultural discourses, their intertextuality and semiotics.

I would like to thank my friends Shubhi and Soup, and niece Meghna for reading and critiquing the early, extremely raw drafts. Akhilesh, a quintessential aesthete for his insights. Simran and Ankit for their secretarial assistance, and Kalikant for feeding me dizzying amounts of food.

Special acknowledgement is due to my post-feminist friend Ruchira for connecting me to Kanishka Gupta, my agent. Adorable and wise, Kanishka has walked me through several grotty reality-check moments. Many hugs are due to my partner, Tripurari, and son, Vivan, for keeping my life real during the emotionally overheated periods of my self-indulgent, three-year romance with the text.

Acknowledgements

I am also grateful to Mriga, Gunjan, Devangana and the entire Penguin Random House team for their support. I am especially grateful to my commissioning editor, Swati Chopra, for dealing with both the anodyne and dramatic side of the publication process with equanimity and charm.

196

Notes

Chapter 1: Born to Dance

1. The names of cities have been intentionally retained as they were known during the time that is sketched in the narrative of this book.

2. Saurashtra, a separate state on the Arabian Sea coast until 1956, is now a part of Gujarat.

3. Poornima spent her time teaching writing skills to Kasturba and other prison inmates. Over time their relationship grew close and intimate, and was cherished by both Kasturba and Gandhiji.

4. Official residences of state governors in India.

5. This was during the Dalai Lama's second visit to India at the invitation of the Mahabodhi Society of India for the 2500th birth anniversary celebrations of Gautam Buddha.

6. Gujarati for 'lovely child'.

7. One of the Indian classical dance forms, it takes its name from the region of its origin, Manipur, a north-eastern state.

8. A gharana is the carrier of several generations of teaching tradition, with its own distinctive style and repertory, in a city—from where a gharana took its name.

9. Earlier known as Coorg, a picturesque district of the state of Karnataka.

10. A dominant style in Indian classical music known for its sensuous melody, rhythm and word meanings explored through intensely expressive variations.

11. A long-necked lute stringed with four or five metal strings, used as accompaniment in classical recitals.

12. A genre of singing where vigorous oscillation is added to each note.

13. M.S. Subbulakshmi is believed to have been bestowed with the title of 'the nightingale of India' by Sarojini Naidu.

14. Vilayat Khan pioneered this style, famously singing the compositions while playing them on his sitar.

15. Melody with a distinct root, mood and movements.

16. A popular, traditional sport in India.

17. Another popular, traditional sport, also known as *sadugudu*, *pattaikodu*. It received its first international exposure during the Berlin Olympics in 1936.

18. Modelled on the lines of London's red double-decker services, the BEST double-decker is now seen as part of the 'heritage' of Mumbai, restricted to a few routes around south Mumbai.

19. An annual celebration of the birth of the Hindu deity, Krishna.

20. A traditional headwear.

21. A traditional, unstitched male garment wrapped around the waist.

22. Ornate, silver-coloured, horse-drawn, open carriages, dating back to Queen Victoria's reign.

23. Bharatha K. Iyer, *Kathakali: The Sacred Dance-Drama of Malabar* (London: Luzac and Company, 1955).

24. Food cooked in the Saurashtra region of Gujarat with seasonings like mustard seeds, pounded red chillies, cumin and coriander.

25. A very important part of Gujarati cuisine.

26. Silks woven in the ancient town of Kanchipuram in South India.

27. An Indian art and cultural historian. An innovator in the field of museology, he is the trustee–director of Sanskriti Foundation.

28. Musical compositions that require graceful movements and emotions.

29. One of the world's greatest dancers, she was a leading Bharatanatyam exponent.

30. *Kaka* is a term endearingly used for father's brother or for someone akin to that status.

31. Sangam is the confluence of three rivers Ganga, Yamuna and the mythic Saraswati. The point of confluence is a revered place for Hindus.

Chapter 2: The Bharatanatyam Years

1. A rhythm-beating, short, wooden stick used for teaching.

2. The art of expression, a key dimension of Indian classical dances.

3. Vedas are ancient texts of Hinduism. There are four Vedas, with the oldest of the four Vedas, Rig Veda, composed around 1500 BC and codified around 600 BC.

4. In Tamil, the term used was *devaradiyal* or 'at the feet of God'. Another popular term was *nitya sumangali*, an ever-auspicious woman. Even though ritually wedded to a deity, she was allowed to enter into liaisons with men and procreate.

5. An expert musician and choreographer who sings and plays the cymbals and conducts a dance recital.

6. The term nautch was used by the Victorians to describe 'dancing girls' whom they regarded as prostitutes.

7. In Tamil, stage is *aranga*, and *etram* connotes climbing.

8. The Devadasi Act declared the performing of any dance by any woman in the precincts of any temple or religious institution or, in any procession of a deity, unlawful.

9. Dancers like Ruth St. Denis, Anna Pavlova and Uday Shankar played a role in the revival by kindling much more than a voyeuristic interest in India's traditional dance forms in the international arena.

10. Calling it a momentous occasion, both for her and for the history of dance in India, Leela Samson quotes from a Madras daily that reported the event: 'Her recital was the single most important event that created a new climate of appreciation in the minds of the people and gave rebirth and an unparalleled stimulus to the recognition of this form of dancing as a prime treasure of Indian culture.' (Leela Samson, *Rukmini Devi: A Life* (New Delhi: Penguin Books India, 2010), p. 89)

11. The linear format that all Bharatanatyam dancers are mandated to follow.

12. At the centre of a Bharatanatyam recital, varnam is abstract and expressive.

13. An expressive dance around the theme of love and the pain of separation from the beloved, symbolic of the soul's yearning for union with the divine.

14. The *guru-shishya parampara*, or teacher–disciple tradition, is a deeply embedded cultural tradition in India. A guru is seen as spiritual mentor. According to scholars, the initiation of a new entrant into the parampara was akin to baptism into Indian cultural citizenship.

15. Balasaraswati had residencies at universities and arts organizations during her global tours.

16. The techniques of Bharatanatyam or the *banis* were defined by the notion of individual aesthetic choices. The Pandanallur Bani was shaped by Meenakshisundaram Pillai.

17. Jayalakshmi Alva trained later with Swarnasaraswati and Mylapore Gowri Ammal.

18. A classical style of Persian/Arabic origin that gathered momentum in the eighteenth century.

19. An Urdu word for practice.

20. An iconic Indian actress.

21. The word *alarippu* connotes blooming. It is a short dance, designed to set up the technical framework and provide a base for succeeding items. *Tillana* occurs at the end of the recital. Sonal calls it 'a pure dance extravaganza exhibiting the exciting possibilities of rhythm-bound vagaries'.

22. Love or *Eros*, one of the primary emotions used in Indian performing arts.

23. 'The Lasting Tradition of the Guru–Shishya Parampara', *Asian Age*, 24 February 2014.

24. Sequences of drum syllables.

25. Musical notes.

26. As reported in 'Delightful Dance Recitals', *Deccan Herald*, 21 June 1961.

27. The art of expression that relates to body movements.

28. The art of expression that relates to emotional states.

29. *Purulia Chhau* is a variation of the Chhau dance performed in West Bengal using colourful masks representing characters

from the epics, the Puranas and from mythology. The mask in Sonal's living room is that of the Hindu goddess Bhagwati, an incarnation of the Hindu goddess, Durga.

30. 'New Slant to Dance Recital Pleases', *Indian Express*, 1 January 1963. The *ashtapadi*s are Sanskrit hymns or couplets grouped into eights, composed in the twelfth century by the famous Indian poet, Jayadeva.

31. A work in Sanskrit by poet Bilvamangala Swami.

32. As reported in 'Sonal Shines in Dance Recital', *Times of India*, 12 March 1963.

33. *Rasa* in broad terms can be described as aesthetic relish. It is a very important term in Indian dance aesthetics. The celebrated 'aphorism on rasa' is found in Chapter 6 of the *Natyashastra*. As Bharata explains, rasa emanates from the conjunction of *vibhava* (factors), *anubhava* (reactions) and *vyabhicharibhava* (transitory emotions). Bhakti connotes devotion.

34. The text of Balasaraswati's presidential address at the 33rd Annual Conference of the Tamil Isai Sangam, delivered on 21 December 1975, translated from Tamil by S. Guhan, is part of the Institutional Archives at the National Centre for the Performing Arts, Mumbai.

35. An ornate entrance to a temple.

36. The first dance piece that a Bharatanatyam dancer learns and performs.

37. The intermediary space between the temple exterior and the sanctum sanctorum.

38. The second (non-expressive) item in a Bharatanatyam performance.

39. A pillared hall used for rituals.

40. The third item in a Bharatanatyam recital using alternating sequences of expressive and abstract dance.

41. A dance that was once performed in the temples and courts of Andhra Pradesh and other Telugu-speaking regions of South India.

42. A traditional theatre style found in Karnataka that integrates dance, music and narration.

Chapter 3: The Journey to Odissi

1. In Sonal's words, the alarippu is designed to set up the technical framework which provides a base for the succeeding items. It is danced to rhythmic syllables uttered by the *nattuvanar*, reproduced on the cymbals and percussion instruments. The more complicated dance patterns and rhythms come in the form of jatiswaram. The third item is sabdam, song with four verses, each giving a dancer the scope to bring out a few interpretations. Varnam is poetry in dance. The text of a varnam usually comes from classical literature and reflects their emotional and philosophical richness. The source material is from the time-honoured epics, Puranas and the works of saints and poets. A working knowledge of Sanskrit, Tamil, Telugu and Kannada is, hence, essential. Padams are songs that require a more languid pace of rendering of expressions and emotions. Own interpretations play an important role in the unfolding of emotions. Tillana occurs at the end of the recital. It's a pure dance extravaganza exhibiting possibilities of rhythm-bound vagaries. The concluding cadences of a tillana draw arc-like movements, criss-crossing the stage and bringing a Bharatanatyam recital to an end with rapid-fire dance movements.

2. The honorarium amount was woefully inadequate. Sonal had to meet the travel cost of her entourage of four musicians from Bangalore, their local stay, their fees, and her own travel cost

from Bombay! Much of the combined expense was met from meagre savings from earlier recitals.

3. 'Damayanti Excels in Kathak', *Indian Express*, 9 October 1964.

4. Michael Ondaatje, an acclaimed novelist and poet.

5. Raja Ravi Varma, a renowned nineteenth-century artist from the royal family of Travancore.

6. The Hathigumpha inscription in Udayagiri dating back to second century BC is the earliest available record of one of the earliest possible variants of Odissi dance.

7. Portions of Skanda Purana written during AD tenth and eleventh centuries mention that dance formed a part of the ritual world of Lord Jagannath, a deity worshipped by Hindus.

8. The gotipua dance emerged in the sixteenth century at a time when the Mughals were trying to establish their dominance in Orissa. As a strategy of resistance, *akharas* were constructed to give young boys physical training. When the mahari dance form begun to decline, the temple space was used by boys from akharas to dance and sing. Ramchandradeva, the king of Khurda, encouraged gotipuas to dance before Lord Jagannath on special occasions like the Chandan Jatra celebrated in the hot, summer months of April–May. This was in the 1650s. Towards the end of the nineteenth century, gotipua troupes began to be administered by guru choreographers.

9. An Odissi repertory includes invocation or mangalacharan, a percussion-based nritta item called *sthayi*, followed by *pallavi*. The concluding item is *moksha*, a piece in nritta designed 'as the final homage to creation through dance'—Sonal in *Classical Dances*, Incredible India series (New Delhi: Wisdom Tree, 2007).

10. A standing body position used in Odissi with three bends in the body—at the neck, waist and knee.

11. Jiwan Pani, 'Milestones of Achievement', *Economic Times*, New Delhi, 29 April 1992.

12. Spiritual leader, philosopher and theologian—his work took off from the philosophy of the Upanishads.

13. Spiritual teacher, proponent of the Vaishnava school of Bhakti Yoga.

14. A poet saint, he wrote the epic Ramcharitmanas in Awadhi.

15. A Sanskrit text that belongs to the 'Purana' genre of ancient Indian literature.

16. Also a poet, musician and dramatist. Born in Kashmir, his commentary on *Natyashastra*, 'Abhinav Bharti', is considered seminal in the area of philosophy of aesthetics.

17. Popularly known as Vach, one of the most illustrious female rishis of Rig Veda. Her *sukta* or hymn is addressed to Agni, the fire god.

18. The siddhas of Vajrayana Buddhism were tantric gurus or masters. *Chariya Geeti*s are the songs of siddhas preserved in Indo-Tibetan Buddhist canon. Taken from India to Tibet in centuries following Guru Padmasambhava's travel to Tibet in AD seventh century, they have a rich textual content with concentric layers of metaphors and meanings and deeply moving insights in the realm of metaphysics, tantra and Buddhist philosophy.

19. Orissa has a rare tradition of Paala singing that uses poems of exceptional literary merit. Traditionally, Paala was sung and acted out through the night. Sometimes it takes the shape of a competition between two singers.

20. Based on the life of Sunayana (she of beautiful eyes).

21. Sukuntala—she who has beautiful hair.

22. A sixteenth-century Hindu mystic poet and musician.

23. A late fifteenth-century poet saint who composed multitudes of songs dedicated to Krishna.

24. Recipient of the Sangeet Natak Akademi Award, 2013, he has been closely associated with Sonal since 1973.

25. Playful, erotic compositions that trace their origin to the devadasi tradition.

Chapter 4: In Geneva

1. Boat shuttle taken to cross Lake Geneva.

2. One of the most important ethnographic museums in Switzerland.

3. From notes in Sonal's personal archive.

4. She received rave reviews. In Belgium, a commentator wrote,

> On the occasion of the 'India Week' recently organized in the capital by the Amitiees Inde-Luxemburg the organizers invited the interested persons to a unique and beautiful dancing performance. The charming 23-year old Indian dancer Sonal Mansingh caused bursts of applause with her first-class choreographic performance before a large audience.
>
> The young Indian dancer who has danced since the age of seven under guidance of foremost teachers can undoubtedly be counted among the most important ballerinas in the world. Her pantomime and poise captivated the audience by over-average expressiveness and precision and by manifestation of the most diverse feelings.

Cited in a clipping from *Press Observer*, Bruxelles, 4, from Sonal's personal archive.

Chapter 5: A-45, Pandara Road

1. Nirmala Joshi was also the first secretary of the Sangeet Natak Akademi.

2. A dominant presence in the universe of Kathak, a prominent classical dance known for its swirling movements and pirouettes.

3. One of the oldest music festivals in the country, the festival celebrated its sixty-eighth edition in February 2015.

4. Founded in 1952.

5. 'Splendid Dancing by Sonal Mansingh', *Hindustan Times*, 5 October 1967.

6. 'Exquisite Dances by Sonal', *The Statesman*, 6 March 1968.

7. 14 January 1968.

8. 'Dance, Music Festival Off to Fine Start', *Hindustan Times*, 2 November 1969, Sunday edition.

9. 'Sonal's Dance Wins High Praise', *Amrita Bazar Patrika*, 14 May 1968.

10. A legendary Odissi guru. In addition to setting up his own institution, Nritya Niketan, he also taught at the Gandharva Mahavidyalaya and the Shriram Bharatiya Kala Kendra.

11. A close disciple of Kelucharan Mohapatra for more than four decades, Kumkum Lal teaches and performs Odissi. The house at Lytton Lane was allotted to Kumkum's father, the well-known ICS officer Jagdish Chandra Mathur, who was also an acclaimed Hindi author and playwright. Lytton Lane was later renamed Copernicus Marg.

12. A deity worshipped by Hindus. Most frequently identified with Krishna, Jagannath is considered by many to be the eighth avatar or incarnation of Vishnu, known as the preserver and sustainer of life in Hindu mythology.

13. The text of *Dashavatara* is the opening canto of *Geet Govind*, one of the most loved and widely sung poems. The theme also lends itself to the theory of evolution. The evolution from fish to tortoise, and then in an ascending order, wild boar, man-lion, midget, warrior, heroic king, farmer, Buddha, the enlightened one, finally tapering off with *Kalki*, the destroyer.

14. The episode of Sita's first encounter with Ram described lyrically in poet saint Tulsidas's Ramcharitmanas.

15. A Carnatic music raga.

16. V.V. Prasad, 'Dance of the Seventies', *Hindustan Times*, 29 April 1971. The *Indian Express* dance critic endorsed, 'The abhinaya in the Dashavatara and in the episode from Ramayana was elegantly stylised and highly evocative.'

17. In addition to being a legendary teacher and choreographer, Kelucharan Mohapatra was a brilliant percussionist.

18. The text of *Geet Govind*, available in 3,725 manuscripts in twenty-two Indian scripts, is centred on the illicit, erotic love between Radha and Krishna, illustrative of the yearning of the soul to be united with the divine.

19. A sacred pitcher, topped with a coronet of mango leaves, used in Hindu rituals.

20. 'Melody in Many Styles and Moods and the Grace of Odissi', *The Hindu*, 2 January 1970, Madras edition.

Chapter 6: Scenes from a Marriage

1. Amateur Afghan photographers known for their photoessays about Afghanistan in the 1960s. A professor of electrical engineering, Mohammad Qayoumi became president of a major American university. In 2015, he was appointed the chief adviser on infrastructure and technology to the President of Afghanistan.

2. Known as the *Khudai Khidmatgars*, or servants of god, Khan Abdul Ghaffar Khan's unarmed army of Pashtuns played an important role in the anti-colonial struggle. Their commitment to non-violence had its roots in the Pashtun code of ethics and Islam.

3. A prominent raga in Carnatic music known for its pronounced ornamentations. It's a published composition from the anthology of the Tanjore Quartet.

4. An English daily published from Kolkata that stopped publication in 1982.

5. A Puranic legend from the Bhagavata Purana, an ancient religious text.

6. Characters from the epic Mahabharata. When the eldest Pandava lost Draupadi in the game of dice, Dussasana tried to disrobe her in the court of Hastinapur.

7. Drum-like percussion instruments used for rhythmic accompaniment. The ghatam is a clay pot beaten by bare hands.

8. 'Sonal Shines Again', *The Statesman*, 27 April 1971. Lalita Sastri and Kelucharan Mohapatra conducted the Bharatanatyam and Odissi portions of her recital.

9. A 1973 Swedish television drama written and directed by Ingmar Bergman that chronicles love, turmoil, infidelity and divorce in the lives of its two main protagonists, Marianne (Liv Ullmann) and Johan (Erland Josephson).

Chapter 7: New Beginnings

1. A term used for son-in-law.

2. *Geet-Prakash* was written by Krishnadas Badajena Mohapatra in the sixteenth century. Pandit Purusottama's *Sangeeta Narayana* followed sometime in the eighteenth century.

3. A traditional part of the Odissi repertory, danced as the final homage to creation.

4. 'Milestones of Achievement', an assessment of Sonal's creative work by Jiwan Pani in the *Economic Times*, New Delhi, 29 April 1992.

5. Mayurbhanj was a large princely state in Orissa where the royal family was the chief patron of this dance form.

6. There is an interesting description of her predicament in an article in *India Today*:

> In the years immediately following her separation, Mansingh was locked into a Kafkaesque dance with the Indian bureaucracy. She and her husband had lived at the government-subsidised Curzon Road apartments in New Delhi. She had applied for the flat to be transferred to her name after her estranged husband went abroad. For months the Government kept her in limbo with your-case-under-consideration run-arounds. Suddenly, without notice, the Government evicted her and charged her market rent, penalty rent 'and all kinds of other strange things I didn't understand,' she says, for a total of Rs. 14,000 that she had to borrow from friends to pay.

(Inderjit Badhwar, 'Tale of a Dancer', *India Today*, 4 March 2014).

7. A famous Indian art patron, curator and collector who was the chairman of the Indian National Trust for Art and Cultural Heritage (INTACH) for fifteen years. He is the patron of the Sanskriti Foundation, established in the late 1970s.

8. The then cultural adviser, India Tourism Development Corporation, a big influence in the field of culture.

9. A diplomat, appointed as special envoy to the then prime minister Indira Gandhi in 1975.

10. A close associate of Sonal's grandfather, she was a key figure in the cooperative, socialist and feminist movements. She is also remembered for her seminal contribution in reviving the traditional handicrafts and handloom traditions in post-Independence India.

11. A Delhi district court.

Chapter 8: Born Again

1. Sonal Mansingh, 'Why I Am "Dwijaa"—Twice Born', *Asian Age*, 19 August 2014.

2. Describing her predicament in the *Asian Age*, Sonal writes:

> Night and day had become meaningless. 'Why am I alive? I must die and pray before my last breath that I may be born in India again, learning dancing and fulfilling my unfinished *karma* of this birth.' I began refusing food. Within two days, I was as white as the sheet on which I lay. The ceiling of the room became my confidant. My self-deprecations, prayers, questions and taunts were all addressed to that ceiling, where they remained, looking down and mocking me. 'Look at yourself. Dancer! You are a mummy. Don't even dream of dancing. Your life is empty and devoid of joy. Every day you are a burden on others and yourself. Why are you hanging on . . .?' Tears ran down my pale, bony cheeks. Visions of my *gurukula vaasa* (living in the guru's home to learn) in Bengaluru brought momentary relief. I tried doing dance mentally, but the thread would break, as suddenly shooting pain would obliterate every other feeling. The constant refrain in my conscious and subconscious was 'Why me?'

Sonal Mansingh, 'Dwijaa's Struggle Continues', *Asian Age*, 2 September 2014.

3. The basic half-seated, knee-out posture of Bharatanatyam with feet in a V shape and distance of two to three fingers between the heels, that has to be mastered before the initiate can even lift a foot. Also referred to as *aayatam* and *ardhamandalam*.

Chapter 9: The Arc Lights

1. 'According to eye witnesses, it was perhaps her greatest performance, as she had deliberately chosen the most difficult compositions. At the end of it she stood before a public in raptures, tears in her eyes, delighted to have been able to find herself again.'

   Interview with Sonal Mansingh, Sri Aurobindo Ashram, 10 May 1993.

2. A composition based on nine ragas, portraying the navarasas or the nine emotions.

3. Cited in Inderjit Badhwar, 'Tale of a Dancer', *India Today*, 4 March 2014.

4. Pritish Nandy, 'Prima Donna', *Illustrated Weekly of India*, 3 June 1984.

5. An iconic Hindi writer, author of the acclaimed Hindi novel *Maila Anchal*.

6. A noted Kannada writer who was also a social activist and film-maker. He received the prestigious Jnanpith award in 1977.

7. A poet and playwright, Safdar Hashmi was a Communist Party of India (Marxist) leader and one of the founder members of the Jana Natya Manch (JANAM), an organization that has played a seminal role in the creation of an all-India street theatre movement.

8. It's a well-known traditional theatre form from Karnataka.

9. The Maintenance of Internal Security Act, a draconic law passed by the Indian parliament in 1971 used for quelling dissent. It was repealed in 1977 when Indira Gandhi lost her power.

10. A performance that features a duet of two solo dancers or musicians.

11. A literal translation of this word is not possible. In this context, it has been used to connote a man with discerning taste, a connoisseur.

12. The Special Protection Group for providing proximate security to the President of India, the prime minister, former prime ministers and members of their immediate families.

Chapter 10: Pulling Back the Curtains

1. Author and poet, Mario Benedetti, known for his passionate verses on love, anger and resistance.

2. Swati Gupte Bhise is an acclaimed Bharatanatyam dancer with her own institute in New York. She has performed at many prestigious places like the Smithsonian Institution, the Brooklyn Museum, the Delaware Institute for the Arts in Education, the San Diego Museum and the General Assembly of the United Nations, and has been instrumental in introducing Bharatanatyam in the curriculum of around 300 schools in New York.

3. A congress veteran, he made his Lok Sabha debut in 1972, and later was the Union minister for information and broadcasting in Indira Gandhi's cabinet.

4. Nasir Moinuddin and Nasir Aminuddin Dagar performed together and were known as the senior Dagar brothers or Bandhus. Their younger brothers Nasir Zahiruddin and Nasir Faiyazuddin Dagar also performed together and were known as the younger/junior Dagar brothers.

5. Rakhi is a sacred thread that symbolizes a sister's love for her brother and the brother's lifelong vow to protect her. It is also

used to consecrate the sibling-like ties between a girl and a boy who may not be biologically related.

6. One who is sought-after for worship and for fulfilling spiritual aspirations.

7. The chariyas were set to music selected from the thirteenth-century text, *Sangeet Ratnakar*. One of them is Shoonya Mahari, or 'Dancer in the Living Void'.

8. Sonal Mansingh, 'A Million-Dollar Question', *Asian Age*, 12 December 2014.

9. Sonal Mansingh, 'Draupadi's Essence Is Only Seen in Parts', *Asian Age*, 28 October 2014.

10. He was a state minister thrice, in the governments headed by Jagannath Pahadia, Shiv Charan Mathur and Harideo Joshi, between 1980 and 1993.

11. The Manganiyar and Langa folk musicians dot the Thar Desert of Rajasthan. Their dialect may be the same, but their repertory differs.

12. The Berlin Akademie der Künste, founded in 1696, is an international community of artists that promotes visual arts, architecture, music, literature, performing arts, film and media art.

13. Located between the Nar and Narayan mountains, Badrinath gets its name from the temple of Badrinath.

14. One of the most sacred stotras or prayers of Hinduism that contains a thousand names of Vishnu with their attributes.

15. The names are Vishnu, Janardana, Padmanabha, Prajapati, Chakradhara, Trivikrama, Narayana, Shridhara, Govinda, Madhusoodana, Narasimha, Jalashaayina, Varaha, Raghunandana, Vaamana, Madhava.

16. In Hindu mythology, asuras are defined by their opposition to the devas or *suras* (gods).

Chapter 11: The Personal and the Political

1. A movement steered by the Safdar Hashmi Memorial Trust (SAHMAT) formed in 1989, soon after Safdar Hashmi's death, by leading artists, writers, poets, scholars and theatre personalities.

2. Vivek Monterio, reporting for the *Economic Times* on 1 April 1992, wrote:

> The response from the artists as also from the public and the media was tremendous. Tyeb Mehta got up from a very sick-bed, against his doctor's orders, and painted the outstanding blow-up of his traffic leitmotif 'falling figure' for the extensive backdrop of the stage erected for the 12 hour cultural sit-in at Shivaji Park.
>
> After the concert one was left with yet another definition of communalism—it is the richness and variety of our national history and culture . . . To those who are seeking creative ways and means of promoting secularism . . . It established that there are hundreds of modes of integration waiting to be discovered.

3. An Indian, overridingly Hindu, right-wing organization.

4. An eighteenth-century Sufi poet, humanist and philosopher.

5. From 'Yamuna: A Witness to Krishna Leela', *Asian Age*, 5 June 2014.

6. Commenting on Draupadi's relationship with Krishna, Sonal wrote:

> It filled me with a sense of envy. She is his only friend; the rest were wives, beloveds, devotees or admirers. There is a perfect understanding and trust between them. They must

have enjoyed each other's company, indulged in witty conversations and repartees as Draupadi was more than a match for even Krishna. (Sonal Mansingh, *Asian Age*, 28 October 2014).

7. Ashish Khokar, *Times of India*, 10 May 1994.

8. Ashish Khokar goes on to say, 'Mere group compositions become a repetitive exercise in a set mould and more than self-expression, it services self-indulgence. Soloists also lack the ability to hold audience interest for long and seldom know when and where to stop. In all these aspects, Sonal Mansingh triumphs.'

Times of India, 10 May 1994.

9. A 'full sitting' posture in Bharatanatyam. Sitting on toes, heels joined with the toes pointed outward.

10. Leela Venkataraman, *The Hindu*, 6 May 1994.

11. Robin Grove, 'Past and Present Meet in Lavish, Timeless Gestures', *The Age*, 12 July 1996.

12. Lee Christofis, *The Australian*, 12 July 1996.

13. Sabarasa is the composite experience of navarasa, the nine emotions.

14. Donna Nebenzahl, 'The Vocabulary of Motion', *Montreal Gazette*, 1 November 2001.

15. Noh is one of the oldest existing forms of theatre. It grew during the fourteenth century, combining strands of Chinese performing arts, known as *Sarugaku*, with a traditional Japanese dance called *Dengaku*.

16. 29 April, the International Dance Day, also known as the World Dance Day, was established in 1982. Its activities are driven primarily by the Conseil International de la Danse—CID, the official platform for all forms of dance in all countries of the

world. Founded in 1973, it is located within the UNESCO headquarters in Paris.

17. A non-profit organization, that began as the Asia Pacific Dance Alliance in Hong Kong in 1988—with two regional centres, WDA Asia-Pacific and WDA Americas.

18. One of the primary anchors of NDTV 24x7 news show.

19. Translated into English, this would mean humanity. Sonal's group connected it with the process of looking within one's soul.

20. Sonal Mansingh, *Classical Dances*, Incredible India Series (New Delhi: Wisdom Tree, 2007).

21. This dance form from Assam was introduced in the fifteenth century AD by saint and reformer Sankaradeva. It was nurtured by vaishnava *math*s or monasteries known as *sattra*s.

22. The Bharatiya Janata Party (BJP) led National Democratic Alliance headed by Atal Bihari Vajpayee as the prime minister.

23. These included Kavalam Narayan Panikkar, Balamurli Krishna and Savitri Heisnan.

24. 'Drama within the Akademi', *Frontline*, Vol. 22, no. 10, 7–20 May 2005.

25. The spiritual head of one of India's renowned spiritual institutions.

26. Saga Dawa is the most important festival in Tibet, held in celebration of Buddha's enlightenment.

27. 'She was always among the top dancers of the country, but Sonal Mansingh was literally the topmost dancer in a literal sense.' 'Reaching the Pinnacle', *The Hindu*, 11 August 2006.

28. A prestigious arts award presented annually by the government of Madhya Pradesh in India.

29. According to Sonal, 'This *shaktipeeth* is one of the oldest fifty-one shaktipeeths or shrines dedicated to the great goddess Devi, and the temple perched on the Nilachal hill in Guwahati, Assam, houses her several manifestations—Kali, Dhumavati, Matangi, Bagalamukhi, Tara, Kamala, Bhairavi, Chhinnamasta, Bhuvaneshwari and Tripura Sundari.'

   The first reference to the place can be found in the inscriptions of the era of Emperor Samudragupta, the second Gupta emperor who ruled from about c. 330 to c. 380 CE. The present temple was built in 1665 by King Naranarayan of Cooch Behar, then a princely state.

30. A Hindi word for someone who is a darling of the gods.

Chapter 12: A New World Coming into View

1. The oral tradition of Vedas that was transmitted as shruti (that which is heard) and smruti (that which is remembered).

2. 'Drowning in Krishna.' In Sonal's words,

   > I opened a new chapter in my career with the offering of Naatya Katha, one of the oldest forms of engagement with people through the re-telling of epic and puranic stories embellished with songs and shlokas in many Indian languages appropriate to the flow of narratives. Having trained as a classical dancer how could I not express my own understanding and interpretations with the touch of a mudra (hand-gesture) or the lift of an eyebrow?

   See: Sonal Mansingh, 'Naatya Katha', *Kalakshetra Journal* 5 (2016): 68.

3. Sonal's friend, chairman and managing director of Mayar, a corporate global organization.

4. A town in the Mathura district of Uttar Pradesh, standing on the bank of the river Yamuna. Vrindavan is synonymous with the stories of Krishna.

5. Composed in Sanskrit. One of the most important classics describing the life and times of Krishna.

6. Eight devotional sixteenth-century poets who composed and sang for Krishna.

7. The musical text is drawn from Sanskrit, Hindi, Avadhi, Braja, Gujarati, Oriya, Kannada and Telugu as required.

8. A traditional stole draped over the shoulders. This description is part of Sonal's essay on naatya katha written for the *Kalakshetra Journal* in 2016.

9. Writing for *The Hindu* after watching Sonal perform at Kalakshetra, Rupa Srikanth adds, 'The Katha, story, went beyond the Kathakaar, the storyteller. Sonal's absolute mastery over music, poetry and philosophy brought Krishna alive.' See: Rupa Srikanth, 'A Colourful Katha', *The Hindu*, 3 March 2016.

10. The founder of non-dualistic philosophy, Adi Shankaracharya has explained that it is only when Shiva is united with Shakti does he acquire the capability of becoming the lord of the universe. In the absence of Shakti, he is shava, akin to a dead body.

11. A decisive figure in the development of twentieth-century hermeneutics.

12. According to some scholars, Nandikeshvara may have preceded Bharata. The *Abhinayadarpan* certainly remains one of the most important sources on classical Indian dance with an overriding focus on the significance of abhinaya.

13. Speaking to the *Hindustan Times* correspondent, Sonal explained, 'It is a strategy for me to bridge the schism between the popular

and pure arts. I hope the show doesn't only let the country discover new talents, but also discover dance in its diversity, richness and beauty.' See: 'Bharat Ki Shaan—A Unique Reality Show from DD', *Hindustan Times*, 14 October 2013.

14. Knowledge or wisdom from the guru as part of the traditional guru–shishya parampara.

15. 'I was more than a mere Sutradhaar,' commented Sonal. 'I wrote out my commentary in long hand in the studio before recording, the final piece fell into place. I was that one character in every episode who saw, predicted and knew the outcome.' See: 'When the Gods Meet, Humans Learn', *Asian Age*, 11 November 2011).

16. A western dance maestro and Bollywood choreographer.

17. 'The last episode was so breath-taking with its splendour and joint wedding ceremonies,' writes Sonal, 'that everywhere the audiences would burst into loud rounds of applause later, some of them confessing to tears streaming down the eyes! I can only say, it is bound to happen when the gods meet.' (Sonal Mansingh, *Asian Age*, 11 November 2011).

18. A school in Delhi. The chairperson of the school, Dr Rohini Ahluwalia, is one of Sonal's friends.

19. Sonal was nominated as one of the nine jewels or ambassadors of the Clean India Campaign in December 2014.

20. Better known in India as Janmashtami, a festival celebrating the birth of Lord Krishna.